Fun finding OUT

Written by Neil Morris

Cartoons by Mark Davis

Miles Kelly

PUBLISHING

Projects created by
Ting Morris

Art director
Clare Sleven

Design
Mackerel Design

Cover design
Jo Brewer

Project management
Mark Darling

Artwork commissioning
Lynne French, Susanne Grant, Natasha Smith

Art reference
Lesley Cartlidge, Liberty Newton

Editorial director
Paula Borton

This edition first published in 2001 (originally published in smaller format, 2000) by
Miles Kelly Publishing Ltd
Bardfield Centre, Great Bardfield, Essex CM7 4SL

24681097531

Copyright © Miles Kelly Publishing Ltd 2000

British Library Cataloguing-in-Publication Data
A catalogue record for this book is available from the British Library

ISBN 1-84236-059-0

Printed in Hong Kong

The publishers wish to thank the following artists
who have contributed to this book:
Lisa Alderson/Advocate, Andy Beckett/Illustration Ltd.,
Martin Camm, Kuo Kang Chen, Mark Davis/Mackerel Design,
Mike Foster/Maltings Partnership, Terry Gabbey/AFA,
Richard Hook/Linden Artists, Rob Jakeway,
John James/Temple Rogers, Mick Loates/Linden Artists,
Janos Marffy, Annabel Milne, Tracey Morgan/B.L. Kearley Ltd.,
Terry Riley, Martin Sanders, Mike Saunders,
Guy Smith/Mainline Design, Rudi Vizi,
Mike White/Temple Rogers, John Woodcock.

The publishers wish to thank the following sources
for the photographs used in this book:
Corbis: Page 139 (T/L), 162 (B), 169 (T/R),
187 (T/L), 188 (C), 189 (BL).
Genesis Photo Library: Page 72 (B/L).
Stock Market: Page 158 (L).
All other photographs from Miles Kelly Archives.

e-mail: info@mileskelly.net
visit us at our website: www.mileskelly.net

CONTENTS

AMAZING ANIMALS

The world's wildlife kingdom is full of amazing creatures – from huge elephants that roam the forest and grassland in small herds to tiny ants that live in enormous colonies. All kinds of animals – mammals, reptiles, birds, insects and others – live in the Earth's unique habitats, from wet forests to dry deserts. Some offer great surprises, such as mammals that can fly – bats, and birds that can't – penguins, who spend most of their time in the freezing sea. Have fun finding out about the world's fascinating animals.

MAMMALS

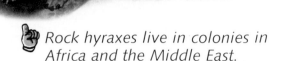

Mammals form a large group of animals. They live all over the world, in hot countries as well as in freezing polar lands. Most mammals live on land, but whales and dolphins are mammals and they live in the sea.

Baby mammals are fed with milk from their mother's body, and an adult mammal has hair or fur to keep it warm.

☝ Rock hyraxes live in colonies in Africa and the Middle East.

Deer and fawn

Mother pig suckling piglets

Factfile

- Farmyard pigs are descended from wild boars.
- There are more than 4,000 different species (or kinds) of mammals.
- The hippopotamus secretes an oily pink fluid which protects it from sunburn.
- Mammals are warm-blooded animals.
- Bats are the only mammals that can fly.
- The pronghorn antelope can sustain a speed of 56 km/h for up to six km.

Hippo

Quiz

1 Are cats and dogs mammals?
2 Which is the largest mammal?
3 Which is the slowest mammal?
4 What is a baby horse called?
5 What are prickly porcupines covered with?
6 Which animal does bacon come from?

Answers
1 Yes. 2 Blue whale. 3 Sloth. 4 Foal. 5 Spines or quills. 6 Pig.

HUMANS ARE MAMMALS TOO!

Mammal mix-up

1. Everyone draws the head of their favourite mammal on a piece of paper. Draw it with a long neck.

2. Everyone folds over the paper, so that only the neck shows, and passes it on to the next player. Without looking under the fold, each player adds a body to the neck.

3. Everyone now folds and passes on. Each player now draws legs and feet/paws and passes on.

4. Now unfold the paper. What's happened to everyone's mammal? What a mix-up!

9

APES & MONKEYS

There are four different kinds of apes. Gorillas and chimpanzees live only on the continent of Africa. Orang-utans and gibbons live in Southeast Asia. Though they are similar to monkeys, apes are larger and have no tails.

There are lots of different monkeys. Many monkeys live in the rainforests of Africa and Asia, alongside apes. The new-world monkeys of Central and South America have long tails, which they use like an extra arm to swing through the trees.

Chimpanzees

Orang-utan

Quiz

1 Which group of animals is closest to man in development?

2 Are baboons apes or monkeys?

3 Which is the smallest ape?

4 What are the world's noisiest monkeys called?

5 Which ape's name means "man of the forest"?

6 Where do snow monkeys live?

Answers

1 Apes. 2 Monkeys 3 Gibbon.
4 Howler monkeys.
5 Orang-utan. 6 Japan.

MORE TEA DR. LIVINGSTONE?

Monkey mobile

1. Make a collection of monkey pictures.

2. Look through old magazines, catalogues, birthday cards, or draw your own monkeys.

COTTON THREAD

COATHANGER

3. Cut them out and stick them on card.

4. Hang the pictures from a wire coat-hanger using cotton thread.

Gibbon

Gorilla

Factfile

- As the world's rainforests are being destroyed, many apes and monkeys are finding it difficult to survive.

- Gorillas are the largest apes; some are the same height as a tall man.

- Chimps use sticks as tools, to dig insects out of their nests.

- A kind of marmoset monkey that had never been seen by people before was found in Brazil in 1996.

- Gibbons can leap distances of up to 15 m between trees.

ELEPHANTS

There are just two different kinds of elephants – African and Asian (which are also called Indian elephants). African elephants are the world's biggest land animals. Males can grow over twice as tall as a man. Asian elephants are smaller and lighter.

Elephants live in family groups, and families often join together to make up large herds. Each herd is led by a female elephant, who is usually the oldest. She decides which route the herd should follow every day.

Factfile

- An elephant's tusks are really two big teeth made of ivory.

- Asian elephants are used in the logging industry, because they can carry very heavy loads.

- Elephants love to wallow in cool mud, which helps to protect their skin.

- Elephants do not have very good eyesight, but their hearing and sense of smell are excellent.

- An African elephant can weigh up to seven tonnes – as much as 90 people.

The African elephant has larger ears than the Asian.

Quiz

1 Can elephants swim?

2 What is the word for a large group of elephants living together?

3 What is an elephant's long, bendy nose called?

4 Which aeroplane is named after an elephant?

5 Do elephants eat meat?

6 What are baby elephants called?

Elephant chain

1. Fold a long sheet of paper backwards and forwards into wide zigzags.

2. Copy an elephant onto the top page of the zigzag, with the tail joined to one edge and the trunk joined to the other.

3. Now cut around the outline carefully.

4. Draw ears and eyes, and colour them in.

5. Open out your elephant chain. All the elephants are holding trunks and tails.

①

② FOLDED PAPER

③

④

⑤

The Indian elephant is an endangered species. There are now less than 40,000 left in the wild.

CATS

Our pet cats at home are relatives of the big cats that live in the wild. All cats are carnivores, which means that they eat meat. They have powerful bodies to help them move fast to hunt their prey. They have excellent eyesight and a good sense of smell.

Most big cats live alone or in pairs, but lions live together in groups, called prides. Male lions like to sit around and let the lionesses do most of the hunting.

In a pride of lions, lionesses spend a lot of time looking after their cubs.

Leopards are the most widespread of the big cats. They can be found in Africa, the Middle East and Asia.

Quiz

1 What are baby tigers called?

2 What does a male lion have around his neck?

3 What noise does a pet cat make?

4 Which big cat lives in the rainforests of Central and South America?

5 Do lions and lionesses look the same?

6 Which is bigger, a tiger or a tigress?

Answers
1 Cubs. 2 Mane. 3 Miaow.
4 Jaguar. 5 No. 6 Tiger.

14

Paper plate cat masks

1. Turn yourself into a big cat with a paper plate and paints. Cut a nose hole and slits for eyes. Paint a cat face – a tiger or a lion.

2. Stick on paper ears and wool whiskers. Yellow and orange crêpe paper strips make a good lion's mane.

3. Make a hole at each side of the plate and loop elastic bands through the holes. Slip the bands over your ears and roar away!

PAPER PLATE

ELASTIC

WOOL WHISKERS

The cheetah is the fastest land mammal over short distances, reaching its top speed of 100 km/h from a standing start in just three seconds.

Factfile

- Tigers are the biggest cats, reaching up to 3.7 m from head to tail.

- Pumas are also called cougars or mountain lions.

- A leopard's spots and a tiger's stripes let them blend in with their surroundings; this is called camouflage.

- A tiger eats about six tonnes of meat a year, which is the same as about 60,000 burgers!

- Most cats avoid water, but tigers like to swim.

BEARS

Bears are big, strong mammals. There are eight different kinds, and most are omnivorous, which means that they eat meat and plants. Brown bears live in forests in North America, Europe and Asia. In America they are usually called grizzlies, and they often live near American black bears. Asian black bears, sun bears, sloth bears and spectacled bears live in different parts of the world. Polar bears live only in the frozen Arctic.

The Polar bear is the only bear which actively preys on humans.

Grizzly bears can run at 50 km/h and weigh up to half a tonne.

Factfile

- The bear's closest relatives are racoons and dogs.

- Polar bears are very strong swimmers and can stay underwater for up to two minutes.

- There are a few wild brown bears still left in the Pyrenees mountains, between France and Spain.

- Spectacled bears, so called after their eye markings, live in the forests of the Andes mountains in South America.

- Many black bears are black, but some have brown, grey or bluish fur.

Quiz

1 Which is the largest kind of bear?

2 Can brown bears stand up on two legs?

3 Which bear is also called a dog bear or a honey bear?

4 What is a polar bear's favourite prey?

5 Where do the largest brown bears live?

6 What food do pandas eat?

Answers

1 Polar bear.
2 Yes. 3 Sun bear.
4 Ringed seals.
3 Kodiak Island. 6 Bamboo.

Bean bear

SEEDS AND BEANS

GLUE

1. Copy this bear on a large piece of strong paper and cut out the shape. You will need PVA glue and lots of beans, seeds, lentils and rice to decorate your bear.

2. Cover a small area of paper with lots of glue and stick on the decorations.

3. Repeat these steps until the whole bear is covered.

4. Let bean-bear dry out overnight and pin him up in your room.

DOGS

Domestic dogs are related to many other members of the dog family, such as wolves, foxes and jackals. The wolf is closest to the pet dog, as you can see if you compare a German shepherd and a grey wolf.

Wolves used to roam over many parts of the northern hemisphere, but much of their territory has been taken over by people.

There are many different kinds of foxes, including the common red fox, the fennec fox of the hot desert and the Arctic fox of the frozen north.

The dingo, the wild dog of Australia, hunts kangaroos, sheep and cattle.

The fennec is the smallest fox but it has the longest ears.

Factfile

- The whole dog family is descended from a wolf-like creature, called Tomarctus, that roamed the world's forests about 15 million years ago.
- The short-legged dachshund, or "sausage dog", used to be trained to hunt badgers.
- The coyote's scientific name, Canis latrans, means "barking dog"; it is well known for its wailing howl.
- The Ancient Egyptians had dogs that looked like greyhounds.

Quiz

1. What is another name for a German shepherd dog?
2. Where would you find coyotes?
3. What is the name of the rescue dog of the Swiss Alps?
4. Which is the smallest fox with the biggest ears?
5. What is the Australian wild dog called?
6. Which breed are the world's tallest dogs?

Answers

1 Alsatian. 2 North America. 3 St Bernard. 4 Fennec fox. 5 Dingo. 6 Great Dane.

Red foxes are found all over Europe, Asia and North America.

Put a tail on the dog

1. Find or draw a large picture of a dog and put it on the wall.

2. Cut out a tail in stiff card and stick a blob of multi-purpose tac at the top.

3. Each player is blindfolded in turn and must stick the tail as close as possible to the right place on the dog.

4. Mark the spot chosen by each player – the closest is the winner.

CARDBOARD TAIL

YAP YAP

GRRRRRRR

Grey wolves live in families and hunt in packs of up to forty.

WHALES & DOLPHINS

Dolphins belong to the same family as whales. Although they spend their whole lives in the sea, whales and dolphins are not related to fish and they cannot breathe under water. They are mammals, and they come to the surface regularly to take in air through a blowhole on the top of their head.

Some whales are huge. The killer whale is nine metres long, and the enormous blue whale is up to 33 m long – the largest animal in the world.

Grey whale and calf

Killer whale

Bowhead whale

ARGGHH!

Quiz

1 What is an aquarium for dolphins called?

2 What colour is a beluga whale?

3 What is a large group of whales called?

4 Which small whale was originally called a "pig fish"?

5 Which South American river has freshwater dolphins?

6 What are baby whales called?

Answers
1 Dolphinarium.
2 White.
3 School.
4 Porpoise.
5 Amazon.
6 Calves.

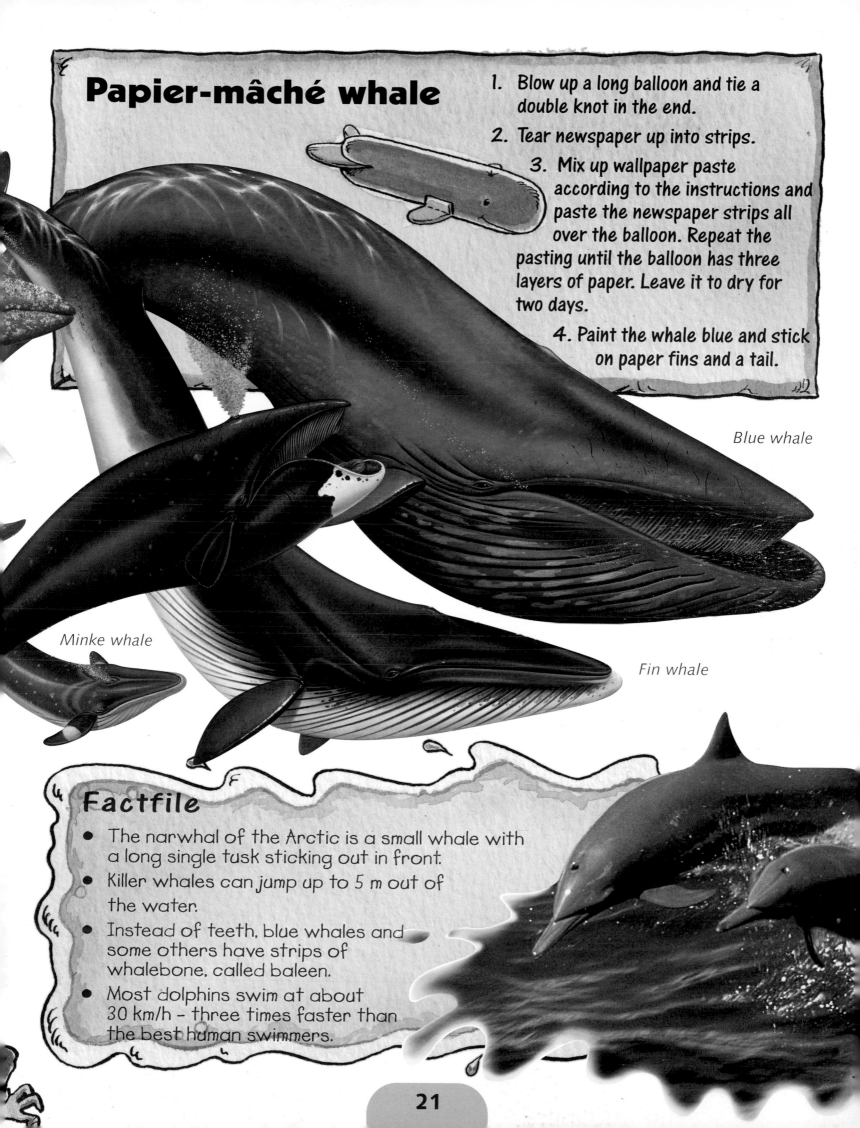

Papier-mâché whale

1. Blow up a long balloon and tie a double knot in the end.
2. Tear newspaper up into strips.
3. Mix up wallpaper paste according to the instructions and paste the newspaper strips all over the balloon. Repeat the pasting until the balloon has three layers of paper. Leave it to dry for two days.
4. Paint the whale blue and stick on paper fins and a tail.

Blue whale

Minke whale

Fin whale

Factfile

- The narwhal of the Arctic is a small whale with a long single tusk sticking out in front.
- Killer whales can jump up to 5 m out of the water.
- Instead of teeth, blue whales and some others have strips of whalebone, called baleen.
- Most dolphins swim at about 30 km/h – three times faster than the best human swimmers.

BATS

There are almost a thousand different kinds of bats. They are all different from other mammals, because they can fly. They live in nearly every part of the world, except for the freezing polar regions.

Most bats are nocturnal, which means that they sleep during the day and come out at night to find food. They hang upside-down to rest and sleep, often from the roof of a cave. Most bats eat mainly insects, but some eat fruit and nectar and others hunt small animals.

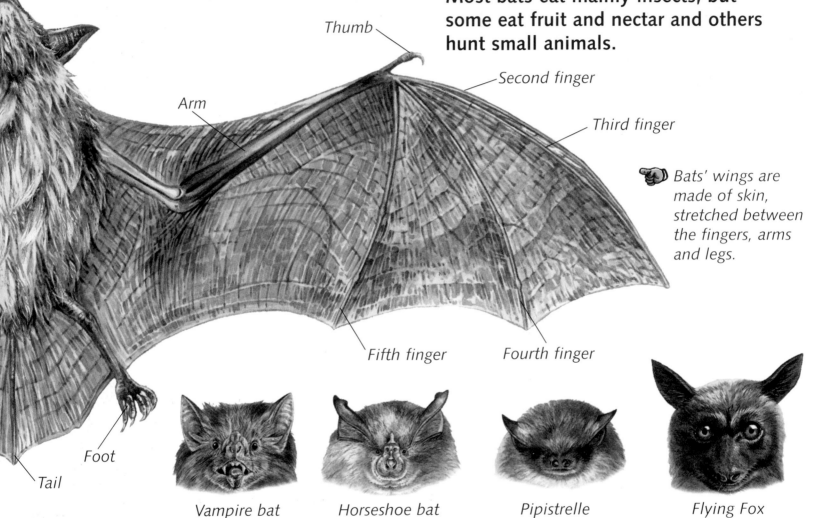

Thumb

Second finger

Arm

Third finger

Bats' wings are made of skin, stretched between the fingers, arms and legs.

Fifth finger

Fourth finger

Foot

Tail

Vampire bat

Horseshoe bat

Pipistrelle

Flying Fox

Quiz

1 What is a blood-sucking bat called?

2 Which is bigger, a bat's body or its wings?

3 Are bats blind?

4 What is the name for a large group of bats that live together?

5 What are bats' wings made of?

6 What is the favourite food of flying fox bats?

Answers
1 Vampire bat 2 Wings.
3 No. 4 Colony 5 Skin. 6 Fruit

Batty bat

1. Fold a piece of card (8 x 28 cm) in half lengthways. Copy the shape of the wing and cut it out. Don't cut the fold.

2. Use a toilet-roll tube for the body and glue pipe-cleaner legs and feelers around it.

FOLDED PAPER

PIPE CLEANER

CURTAIN RING

HOOK

3. Open the wings, tape a curtain ring to the wing, and glue the back of the wings to the body tube.

4. Cut a four metre length of cotton and pass the two ends through the curtain ring. Put the thread over a wall hook and pull your bat towards you along the thread. When the two ends are pulled apart, your bat will go batty.

NYLON THREAD

Bats detect prey using the echoes from their ultrasonic calls and clicks.

Factfile

- In a cave in Texas, USA, 20 million free-tailed bats were found in a single colony.

- Bats use their hook-shaped thumbs to climb trees and rocks.

- Bats use the echoes from their high-pitched squeaks to find their way around.

- They have large sensitive ears to pick up the echoes.

- The fisherman bat of Mexico can catch small fish with its claw-like feet.

- Little brown bats have been found living over a kilometre underground in mines.

MARSUPIALS

Marsupials are a special group of mammals. Unlike all other animals, female marsupials have a pouch. Their babies stay in the warm, snug pouch and live off their mother's milk until they are big enough to leave.

Most marsupials, such as kangaroos, koalas and wombats, live in Australia. Smaller kinds, called opossums, live in North and South America.

☞ Baby kangaroos are called joeys.

☞ The wombat sleeps during the day in its burrow.

☞ Wallabies are like small kangaroos.

☞ Koalas live mostly in trees, eating eucalyptus leaves.

YIKES!

Quiz

1 What is a male kangaroo called?

2 What's special about the water opossum's pouch?

3 What is a kangaroo's main food?

4 Which trees do koalas like best?

5 What does "playing possum" mean?

6 Which kind of rat is named after a marsupial?

Answers
1 Buck. 2 It's waterproof
3 Grass. 4 Eucalyptus.
5 Pretending to be dead.
6 Kangaroo rat.

Factfile

- Kangaroos can jump more than 9 m in one enormous bound.
- Although they look like small bears, koalas have nothing to do with the bear family.
- Male kangaroos sometimes fight each other in a way that looks like boxing.
- Scientists discovered a previously unknown tree kangaroo in Indonesia in 1994.
- The smallest marsupial is the tiny honey possum.

Count the kangaroos

There are five roos hidden in the picture. Can you find them?

REPTILES

Scaly-skinned reptiles are a very different group of animals from mammals because they are cold-blooded. This means that reptiles always need lots of sunshine to warm them up. That is why most of them live in warm parts of the world, and some even live in hot deserts. They go into underground burrows during the hottest part of the day.

Snakes, lizards and crocodiles are all reptiles. Tortoises and turtles are reptiles whose bodies are protected by a shell.

There are more different kinds of lizards than any other sort of reptile.

65 MILLION YEARS AND STILL WE'RE EATING FLIES!

Quiz

1 What kind of reptile is a skink?

2 Where does the giant tortoise live?

3 What colour does an angry chameleon turn?

4 What kind of reptile is a loggerhead?

5 Is the lizard called a gila monster poisonous?

6 What were large prehistoric reptiles called?

Answers
1 Lizard. 2 Galapagos Islands.
3 Black. 4 Turtle. 5 Yes. 6 Dinosaurs.

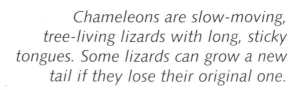

Chameleons are slow-moving, *tree-living lizards with long, sticky tongues. Some lizards can grow a new tail if they lose their original one.*

Walnut turtle

1. Split open some walnuts - each half shell makes a little turtle. If you like nuts, you could make a whole family of turtles.

2. Trace the turtle outline on card and cut it out. Paint the rim of the walnut shell with glue and fit it on the card turtle. Press the rounded part of the shell on the head of your turtle and the pointed end on the tail.

3. Wait for the glue to dry and then paint on eyes and a mouth with black felt pen.

CUT-OUT CARD

WALNUT SHELL

CAMOUFLAGE HAS MANY USES!!

Factfile

- The Komodo dragon of Indonesia, the world's largest lizard, grows up to 3 m long.

- Lizards live on land, but one kind swims in the sea – the marine iguana of the Galapagos Islands.

- Chameleons can change colour to suit their surroundings or their mood.

- The tuatara is a kind of lizard that lives in New Zealand; it belongs to an ancient family related to the dinosaurs.

SNAKES

There are more than 2,000 different kinds of snakes. They are long, legless reptiles that slither and glide forward as their bodies press against roughness in the ground. Some also climb trees, and many snakes can swim.

Snakes have forked tongues, which they flick in and out to pick up scents from the air and ground. Some snakes are poisonous, but only about 300 kinds are dangerous to people.

Poisonous snakes inject venom into their prey through a large pair of hollow teeth called fangs.

King snake

A rattlesnake's rattle is made up of loose scales; the rattler shakes its tail to act as a warning.

Factfile

- The world's longest snake is the reticulated python of Southeast Asia, which grows up to 10 m long.

- Emerald tree boas wrap themselves around rainforest trees and wait for prey such as birds and bats.

- A few snakes give birth to live babies, but most lay eggs with tough, leathery shells.

- One poisonous snake was found to have enough venom in it to kill a quarter of a million mice.

28

Quiz

1 Where does the world's most poisonous snake live?

2 Is a snake's tongue poisonous?

3 Which kind of snake can rear up and spread its hood?

4 How does a boa constrictor kill?

5 Do female snakes look after their young?

6 What is the main colour of a milk snake?

Answers

1 Australia. 2 No. 3 Cobra. 4 By squeezing its victim. 5 No. 6 Red.

A boa constrictor kills its prey by squeezing and suffocating it.

HAVE YOU SEEN MY OTHER SOCK, SON?

Stuffed snakes

1. Cut the legs from an old pair of tights (or use long socks) for two long snakes.

2. Stuff them with crumpled pieces of newspaper and tie the ends.

3. Cut a long forked tongue and two eyes from card or felt and stick them on.

4. Paint coloured stripes or a pattern on your stuffed snakes.

CROCODILES & ALLIGATORS

Crocodiles and alligators belong to a group of reptiles called crocodilians. They are the largest living reptiles. Powerful animals with long tails and fierce jaws, they live close to water and are found mainly in wide rivers and swamps in hot parts of the world. They often bask in the sun during the day.

When it gets dark, they slip into the water to spend the night hunting for fish and other animals.

LOOK OUT, BEHIND YOU!

Quiz

1 Do alligators lay eggs?

2 Which African river has a crocodile named after it?

3 How many different kinds of crocodilians are there – 12, 120 or 1,200?

4 On which continent does the crocodilian called a caiman live?

5 Which ancient people preserved crocodiles as mummies?

6 Which is larger, an American or a Chinese alligator?

Answers
1 Yes. 2 Nile. 3 120. 4 South America. 5 Ancient Egyptians. 6 American.

Crocodiles catch and eat fish, larger mammals and birds.

The long body of a crocodile is covered with thick scales and bony plates along the back for protection.

Cucumber croc

1. Turn a cucumber into a fearsome crocodile. Use cocktail sticks to stick on pieces of carrot for feet and half an olive for each eye.

2. Cut a mouth and hold the jaws open with almond or apple teeth.

3. Croc's scaly back is made of cheese triangles.

CHEESE TRIANGLES

CUCUMBER BODY

OLIVES

CARROTS

ALMOND

ARGGHH!

Factfile

• Crocodiles have narrower jaws than alligators, and when their jaws are closed you can still see teeth sticking out.

• During very hot, dry weather crocodilians may bury themselves in mud and sleep until the weather changes.

• Gavials are crocodilians with long, thin snouts and about a hundred sharp teeth; they live in the big rivers of Malaysia and India.

• The estuarine or saltwater crocodiles of Asia and Australia grow up to 7 m long.

BIRDS

Birds are the only animals with feathers, and their feathered wings make them expert fliers. They live in all parts of the world, and many birds fly long distances at different parts of the year, mainly to find warm weather.

Female birds lay eggs, and most build nests to protect them. When the baby birds hatch out, their parents feed them until the youngsters can fly and safely leave the nest.

☞ *Hummingbirds flap their wings very fast to hover in the air; they use their long beak and tongue to reach for the nectar inside flowers.*

Factfile

- The common swallow breeds in Europe, Asia and North America. Some swallows spend their winter in southern Africa and Australia.

- The Indian peacock can spread its tail feathers into a large, beautiful fan.

- Arctic terns make a round-trip of up to 36,000 km each year, flying between the frozen Arctic and Antarctic regions.

- Common swifts may stay in the air for up to four years, sleeping on the wing.

- The smallest bird is the bee hummingbird of Cuba, which is less than 6 cm long.

Quiz

1. Which bird lays its eggs in the nests of other birds?
2. Which bird runs fastest on the ground?
3. What is the name for a female bird?
4. Which American desert bird is known to run alongside cars?
5. What is the national bird of New Zealand?
6. Which rainforest bird is famous for its long, colourful beak?

1 Cuckoo, 2 Ostrich, 3 Hen, 4 Roadrunner 5 Kiwi, 6 Toucan.

Answers

Birds beat their wings to improve the airflow past their wings. This helps them fly.

The wandering albatross has the biggest wingspan of any bird – up to 3.6 m.

The ostrich is the world's largest bird.

ON YOUR MARKS!

Flying high

1. Make a paper-bag kite. Punch holes 4 cm from the edge of each of the four corners of a large paper bag. Stick paper ring reinforcements on each hole.

2. Cut two pieces of string and tie each end into a hole to make two loops. Tie a long piece of string through the two loops to form a handle.

3. Decorate your kite. Glue on a paper tissue tail.

4. Hold onto the string and run so the wind catches in the bag.

STRING

TISSUE PAPER

PAPER BAG

BIRDS OF PREY

We call birds that hunt animals for food birds of prey. Eagles, hawks and falcons are all daytime hunters. They are fast fliers and have excellent eyesight, so that they can swoop down on their prey from a great height. They grab the victim with their powerful talons and tear it apart with their hooked beaks.

Owls hunt mostly at night, catching small mammals such as mice and voles. Vultures don't normally hunt at all, but live off scraps of dead creatures killed by other animals.

An owl's wing feathers have a soft fringe, which helps the owl fly almost silently and surprise its unsuspecting prey.

Roly-poly owl

1. Make two small holes at the top of an empty yoghurt pot. Push a piece of plastic drinking straw through one side of the pot, through the centre of a cotton reel and out through the other hole of the pot. Fix the ends of the straw with masking tape to stop them slipping out.

2. Cut out six circles (three for each eye) and stick them on the pot. Make wings from pleated sheets of paper, and glue on paper claws and a beak.

COTTON REEL

YOGHURT POT

FOLDED PAPER

Factfile

- The lammergeier, or bearded vulture, drops bones onto rocks to split them open and get at the marrow inside.

- The peregrine falcon is the world's fastest bird; it dives at up to 350 km/h.

- The Egyptian vulture drops stones onto ostrich eggs to crack them open.

- The North American elf owl is just 13 cm long.

- Vultures have been recorded flying at a height of over 11,000 m, as high as a jet plane.

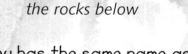

Sharp eyes with excellent long-distance vision

Nostril

Hooked beak, good for tearing meat

Vulture

 Lammergeier dropping bones onto the rocks below

Quiz

1 Which bird of prey has the same name as a flying toy?

2 What is the main food of the osprey?

3 Which eagle is the emblem of the USA?

4 Which is the biggest bird of prey?

5 What was the royal bird of the Middle Ages?

6 Which owl lives near the North Pole?

Answers

1 Kite. 2 Fish. 3 Bald eagle. 4 Condor. 5 Golden eagle. 6 Snowy owl.

ARE YOU SURE THIS WIG WILL STAY ON AT 100 METRES?

PENGUINS

Penguins are birds, but they cannot fly. Their feathers are short and thick, and these help keep penguins warm in cold seas and on frozen shores. Penguins have a small pair of wings, which act as flippers for swimming rather than flying.

They spend much of their time at sea feeding on fish, squid and small shrimp-like krill. Penguins live near the coasts of the cold southern oceans, and many never leave the frozen region of Antarctica.

There are just 3,000 yellow eyed penguins left in the world.

Emperor penguins are the biggest, at up to 120 cm tall.

Quiz

1 What is a baby penguin called?

2 Rockhopper penguins hop from rock to rock – true or false?

3 What is the name of the only African penguin?

4 Are there any penguins at the North Pole?

5 What do penguins use as rudders when they swim?

6 What do we call a colony of penguins?

Answers

1 Chick. 2 True. 3 Jackass penguin.
4 No. 5 Their feet 6 A rookery.

Penguin sock puppet

1. Put your hand into a black sock, so you can work the head with your fingers.

2. Tie or glue a piece of white cloth around the penguin's neck and glue on button eyes.

3. Take the sock off and cut holes on either side. Make a cone beak out of card and attach it with some thread. Push your thumb and little finger through the holes to make the flippers.

Rockhopper penguins have long feathers above their eyes.

Magellanic penguins are found around the freezing coasts of Antarctica.

Factfile

- Emperor penguins put their eggs and chicks on their feet, to keep them warm.

- There are 18 species, or different kinds, of penguin; six species breed in Antarctica, the ice-covered continent around the South Pole.

- The little blue penguin of Australia and New Zealand is the smallest of all, standing 40 cm high.

- Gentoos can swim at up to 27 km/h.

- Penguins sometimes slide along on their body instead of walking; we call this tobogganing.

- Penguins can dive down over 450 m under-water and stay under for 18 minutes.

4,205... 4,206... 4,207... ER.. OH NO! 1, 2, 3, 4.

AMPHIBIANS

Amphibians are animals that spend part of their lives on land and part in water. They include frogs, toads, newts and salamanders. Amphibians go to water when it is time to lay their eggs. Females usually lay their eggs in or near a pond or stream.

Most frogs lay between 1,000 and 20,000 eggs in a mass of jelly. We call these large clusters of eggs spawn. Like many amphibians, frogs go through different stages before they become adults.

① *Frog spawn floats on top of fresh water.*

② *Tadpoles hatch from the eggs.*

④ *The froglet loses its tail and grows into an adult frog.*

③ *Tadpoles grow legs and change into froglets.*

Factfile

- Toads usually have a rougher, bumpier skin than frogs, and they can live in drier places.

- Tree frogs have round suckers on their toes, which help them to grip.

- Big North American bullfrogs can catch mice or even small snakes.

- South American sharp-nosed frogs can jump over 3 m.

I HOPE I DON'T MEET A GIANT SALAMANDER!

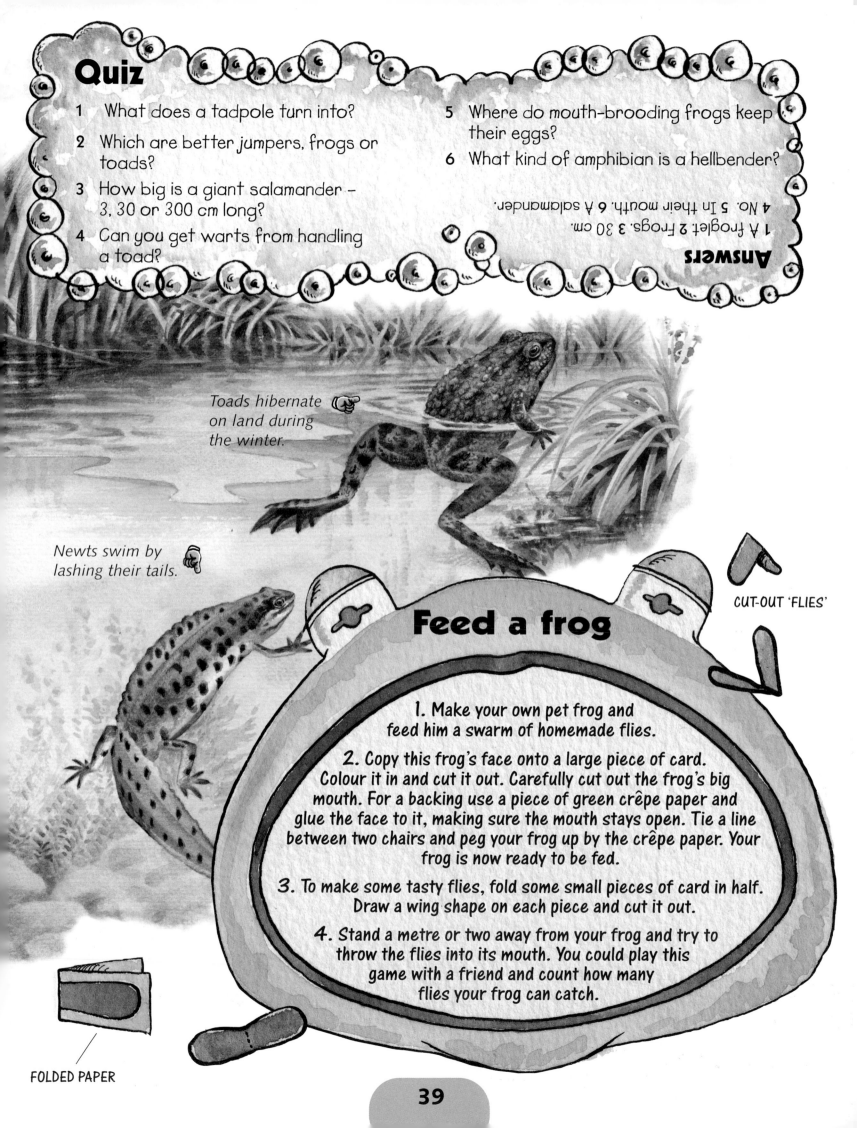

Quiz

1 What does a tadpole turn into?

2 Which are better jumpers, frogs or toads?

3 How big is a giant salamander – 3, 30 or 300 cm long?

4 Can you get warts from handling a toad?

5 Where do mouth-brooding frogs keep their eggs?

6 What kind of amphibian is a hellbender?

Answers

1 A froglet 2 Frogs. 3 30 cm.
4 No. 5 In their mouth. 6 A salamander.

Toads hibernate on land during the winter.

Newts swim by lashing their tails.

CUT-OUT 'FLIES'

Feed a frog

1. Make your own pet frog and feed him a swarm of homemade flies.

2. Copy this frog's face onto a large piece of card. Colour it in and cut it out. Carefully cut out the frog's big mouth. For a backing use a piece of green crêpe paper and glue the face to it, making sure the mouth stays open. Tie a line between two chairs and peg your frog up by the crêpe paper. Your frog is now ready to be fed.

3. To make some tasty flies, fold some small pieces of card in half. Draw a wing shape on each piece and cut it out.

4. Stand a metre or two away from your frog and try to throw the flies into its mouth. You could play this game with a friend and count how many flies your frog can catch.

FOLDED PAPER

39

FISH

There are more than 20,000 different kinds of fish in the world's oceans, lakes and rivers, from the tiniest freshwater minnow to the biggest ocean-going shark. Fish have gills instead of lungs, which allow them to breathe underwater.

Eels have snakelike bodies and very small fins.

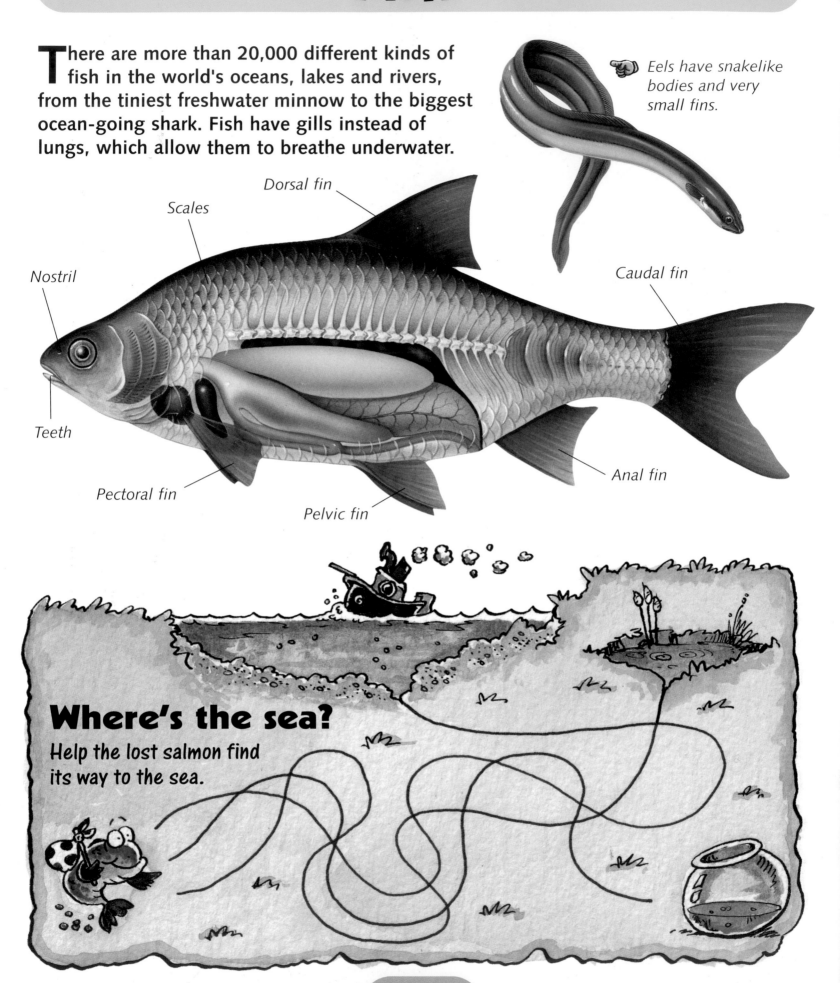

Dorsal fin

Scales

Nostril

Teeth

Pectoral fin

Pelvic fin

Caudal fin

Anal fin

Where's the sea?

Help the lost salmon find its way to the sea.

QUICK LEGGIT!

Quiz

1 Which are real fish – catfish, dogfish, parrotfish?

2 Which South American meat-eating fish has the strongest, sharpest teeth?

3 Which is not a trout – brown, rainbow, sockeye?

4 To which fish family does the goldfish belong?

5 A kipper is a smoked what?

6 Which special food comes from the sturgeon?

Answers

1 All of them. 2 Piranha. 3 Sockeye (it's a salmon). 4 Carp. 5 Herring. 6 Caviar.

Flying fish have pectoral fins shaped like wings.

Rays have flat bodies, which help them glide along the bottom of the sea.

Factfile

- The fastest fish is the sailfish, which can swim at over 100 km/h.

- The porcupine fish swells up into a spiny ball when it senses danger nearby.

- Rays feed mainly on shellfish, which they crack open with their strong teeth; some rays can sting with their tails.

- Electric eels kill fish and other sea animals with electric shocks from their tail.

- Flying fish have large pectoral fins, which they use to jump out of the water and fly for a distance of up to 150 m.

CLOSER... CLOSER... THAT'S IT!

SHARKS

People are fascinated by sharks. They are very frightened of them, too, though many sharks are quite harmless. Nevertheless, sharks are the fierce hunters of the world's oceans. They have big, strong jaws and teeth, and when they attack other fish or dolphins, they show amazing speed and power.

Unlike other fish, a shark's skeleton is made of rubbery cartilage instead of bone. Sharks also do not have a swim bladder, which means they have to keep swimming all the time, or they sink to the bottom.

☞ *The great white shark, famous as "Jaws", normally grows up to 6 m long.*

Starry Smoothhound

Chase the shark

A racing game for two players.

1. Cut out two tissue-paper sharks. Each one should be about 30 cm long. Stick on eyes.

2. Lie the sharks flat on their backs. Place two plates about three metres away on the other side of the room. Hit the ground just behind the shark with a rolled-up newspaper to make it move. The shark that lands on the plate first is the winner.

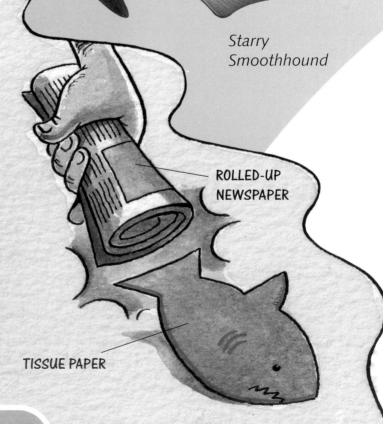

ROLLED-UP NEWSPAPER

TISSUE PAPER

Sandbar shark

☝ The blue shark is a slender fish, with very long pectoral fins and a pointed snout.

Quiz

1 Which shark has a tail as long as its body?

2 Which one does not exist – basking shark, lion shark, or tiger shark?

3 How many gill slits do most sharks have?

4 A dogfish is a small shark – true or false?

5 Are hammerhead sharks dangerous to people?

6 How many different kinds of sharks are there – 25, 125 or 250?

Answers 1 Thresher shark. 2 Lion shark. 3 Five. 4 True. 5 Yes. 6 250.

43

Factfile

• Some female sharks lay eggs in a tough case which we call a mermaid's purse.

• The whale shark is the world's biggest fish, growing over 12 m long, but it is not at all dangerous.

• The world's smallest shark is the dwarf shark, which is just 15 cm long.

• Sharks have an excellent sense of smell and good hearing, which helps them in their hunting.

• The wobbegong, or carpet shark, lies flat and camouflaged on the bottom of the sea.

INSECTS

There are more than a million different kinds of insects in the world. This group of tiny animals accounts for over three-quarters of all animal species on Earth, and more insects are being discovered and named all the time. Insects have no backbone, but are protected by a hard outer skeleton or shell. All insects have six legs, and most have wings and can fly.

Because they are so small, insects can fit into tiny spaces and need little food to live on.

Antennae, or feelers, detect movements of the air, vibrations and smells.

Compound eyes are made up of hundreds of tiny lenses.

Legs and wings are attached to the thorax.

The large abdomen contains many of the insect's organs, such as the heart.

Termites build huge mounds as nests for their colony. Each colony is ruled by a king and a queen.

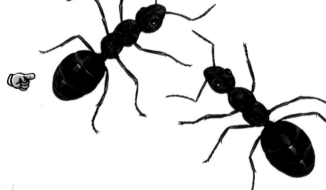

Ants have very strong jaws and can give a painful bite. Some kinds squirt formic acid into the wound made by their bite, adding to the effect!

 Ants live in colonies, which may contain up to 100,000 insects.

Factfile

- Wasps and other insects usually sting to defend themselves and their nests.

- Other insects, such as mosquitoes, are bloodsuckers; they stick a needle-like tube into the skin and suck up a tiny amount of blood.

- A single bee would have to visit more than 4,000 flowers to make one tablespoon of honey.

- When they grow into winged adults, mayflies may live for no more than an hour.

- The fastest flying insects have been timed at 39 km/h.

Honey bees collect nectar and pollen from flowers. They take this food to their nest, where it is stored as honey.

Tissue bugs

1. Screw up tissue paper into a tight ball. Wrap the ball into another piece of tissue paper and hold it together with sticky tape. Paint on eyes and tape on pipe cleaner legs.

2. Paint the ladybird's body red and add black spots. Paint three pipe cleaners black and tape them on to make three legs on each side.

3. You could make other bugs in the same way.

COME ON... BEDTIME WAS OVER 20 MINUTES AGO.

Quiz

1 What kind of insect is a ladybird?
2 Which mosquitoes "bite", male or female?
3 Which insect is called a white ant?
4 How many pairs of wings do most insects have?
5 What are animals without a backbone called?
6 Which insects jump furthest?

1 Beetle. 2 Female. 3 Termite. 4 Two.
5 Invertebrates. 6 Fleas.

Answers

BUTTERFLIES

Like many insects, butterflies change their bodies as they develop. These changes are called metamorphosis.

Butterfly eggs develop into caterpillars. Each caterpillar turns into a chrysalis, and the final stage is a beautiful butterfly. Butterflies have thin, delicate wings, and most are brightly coloured. They usually fly about and feed during the day.

Most moths have a duller colour and fly at night.

Female butterflies *lay their eggs in a batch on a plant. Each egg hatches into a butterfly.*

Caterpillars feed *on the leaves of a plant. Then they turn into a chrysalis, or pupa, which often hangs from a plant.*

Caterpillar

Egg

Chrysalis

Fully formed butterfly

Emerging butterfly

 When the butterfly first emerges from the chrysalis, its wings are soft and crumpled.

Butterfly prints

- Drop blots of different coloured paint in the middle of a sheet of paper. Fold the paper in half and press it down.

PAINT BLOBS

FOLDED PAPER

- Open up the folded paper and admire your butterfly.

- Cut the butterfly out and hang it on your wall. Now it won't fly away!

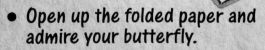

Factfile

- The caterpillar stage of a butterfly is its larva; we often call insect larvae grubs or maggots.

- The world's largest butterfly is the Queen Alexandra's birdwing, which has a wingspan of more than 28 cm.

- The smallest butterflies have a wingspan of just 6 mm.

- When a butterfly rests, it holds its wings upright; a moth folds its wings flat over its body.

- Monarch butterflies have been found to travel more than 3,000 km; some butterflies fly all the way across the Atlantic Ocean.

Quiz

1 Are male and female butterflies always the same colour?

2 What do clothes moth larvae love to chew?

3 What is a butterfly's feeding tube called?

4 Is the red admiral a butterfly or a moth?

5 Which is not a moth – old lady, moon, swallowtail?

6 What colour is a cabbage butterfly?

Answers
1 No. 2 Wool. 3 Proboscis. 4 Butterfly. 5 Swallowtail (it's a butterfly). 6 White.

Antennae

Compound eyes

ONLY TWO MORE STAGES AND YOU'LL BE ABLE TO FLY!!

Upper wing

Lower wing

SPIDERS

Spiders are similar to insects, but they belong to a different group of animals called arachnids. All arachnids have eight legs. Many spiders spin silky webs, which they use to catch flies and other small insects. Spiders have fangs for seizing their prey, and most paralyze their victims with poison before they kill and eat them. Fortunately, only a few spiders are poisonous to humans.

1. The spider's silk comes from inside its body. The spider starts a web by building a bridge.

2. Then it makes a triangle shape.

3. It adds more threads to make a complete framework.

4. Finally, the spider fills the frame with circular threads.

5. A spider's web is strong enough to catch large insects, but it is easily damaged by larger animals and people.

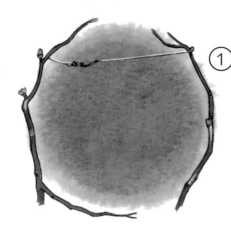
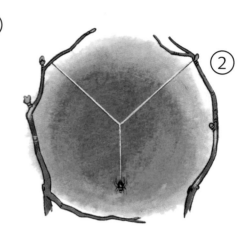

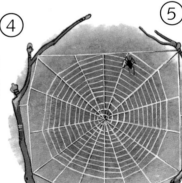

Factfile

- Scorpions, ticks and mites are also arachnids.
- Most spiders and other arachnids have eight eyes, but they still don't see very well.
- In a grassy meadow, there may be as many as 500 spiders in a square metre.
- Female spiders lay up to 2,000 eggs, which they wrap in a bundle of silk threads.
- The world's largest spider is the goliath bird-eating spider of South America, which has a leg span of 28 cm.

Quiz

1 How many more legs has a spider got than an ant?

2 What are baby spiders called?

3 Which golden orb-web spider weighs more, male or female?

4 Where is a scorpion's sting?

5 How many different kinds of spiders are there – 400, 4,000, or 40,000?

6 What colour is the ----- widow spider?

Answers
1 Two more. 2 Spiderlings.
3 Female (about 1000 times more!) 4 In its tail. 5 40,000.
6 Black.

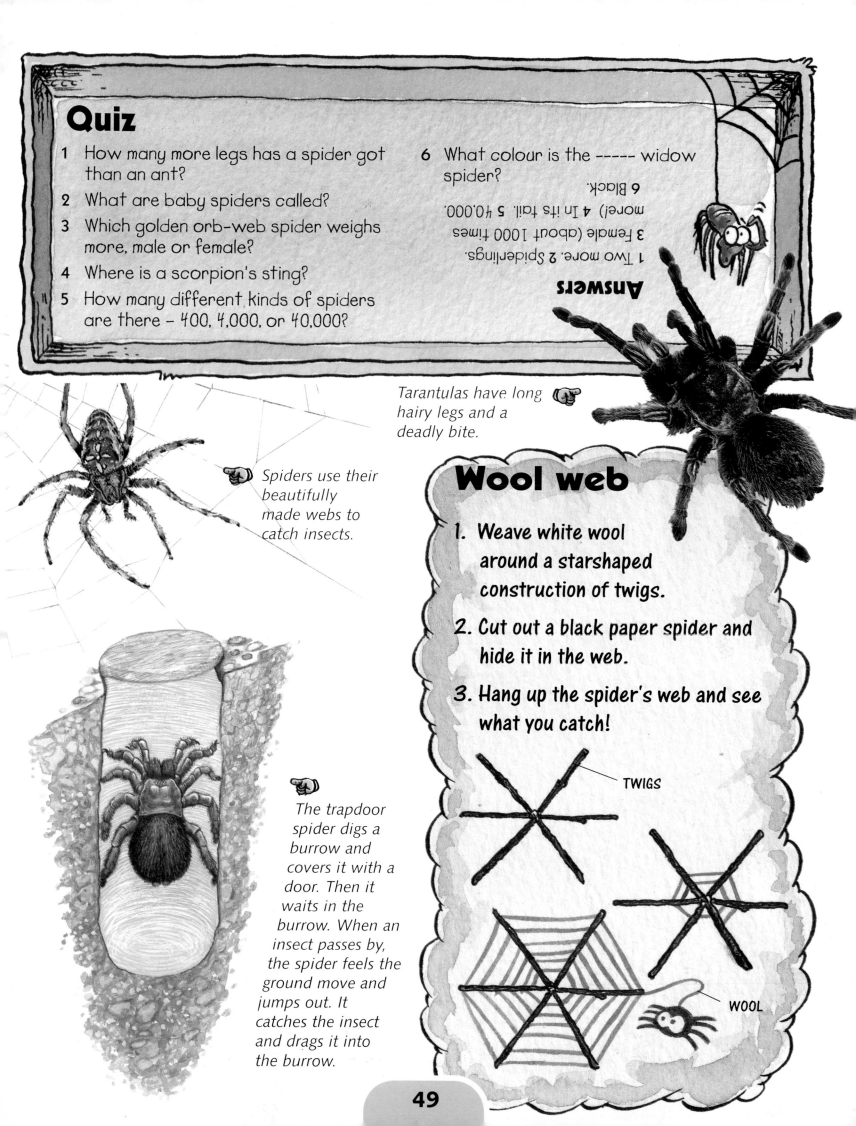

Tarantulas have long hairy legs and a deadly bite.

Spiders use their beautifully made webs to catch insects.

Wool web

1. Weave white wool around a starshaped construction of twigs.

2. Cut out a black paper spider and hide it in the web.

3. Hang up the spider's web and see what you catch!

TWIGS

WOOL

The trapdoor spider digs a burrow and covers it with a door. Then it waits in the burrow. When an insect passes by, the spider feels the ground move and jumps out. It catches the insect and drags it into the burrow.

49

MOLLUSCS & CRUSTACEANS

Many molluscs live in the sea, but some live on land. Many marine molluscs, such as the octopus, have soft bodies. Others, such as land and sea snails, and shellfish such as cockles, mussels and oysters, are protected by hard shells.

Crustaceans got their name from their crusty covering. Most of them, such as crabs, lobsters and shrimps, live in the sea. A few crustaceans, such as woodlice, live on land.

Octopus

Squid

Hermit crab

Modelling dough creatures

1. Use different coloured modelling dough or make your own with two cups flour, one cup salt, one tablespoon cooking oil, one cup water (with added food colouring).

2. Mix the flour and salt, then add the oil and water. Knead well.

3. Roll out a sausage shape for a snail, use two matchstick ends for its tentacles. Mould a crab and an octopus.

Factfile

- Squids and octopuses shoot out inky fluid to cloud the water when they want to get away from enemies.

- The largest crustacean is the giant spider crab, which has a leg-span of almost 4 m.

- The smallest crustaceans are water fleas, which measure less than 0.25 mm.

- Octopuses can change colour according to their surroundings, so they can easily hide.

- The largest bivalve shellfish is the giant clam, which grows up to 115 cm long.

Quiz

1 What does a snail have that a slug doesn't?

2 Do crabs walk frontwards, backwards or sideways?

3 How many legs does a shrimp have?

4 Is a cuttlefish a fish, a mollusc or a crustacean?

5 Which valuable gems grow in oysters?

6 Are there more kinds of land snails or sea snails?

Answers
1 A shell. 2 Sideways.
3 Ten. 4 Mollusc. 5 Pearls.
6 Sea snails.

Lobster

Snail

HOW ABOUT A BIT OF ARMED COMBAT?

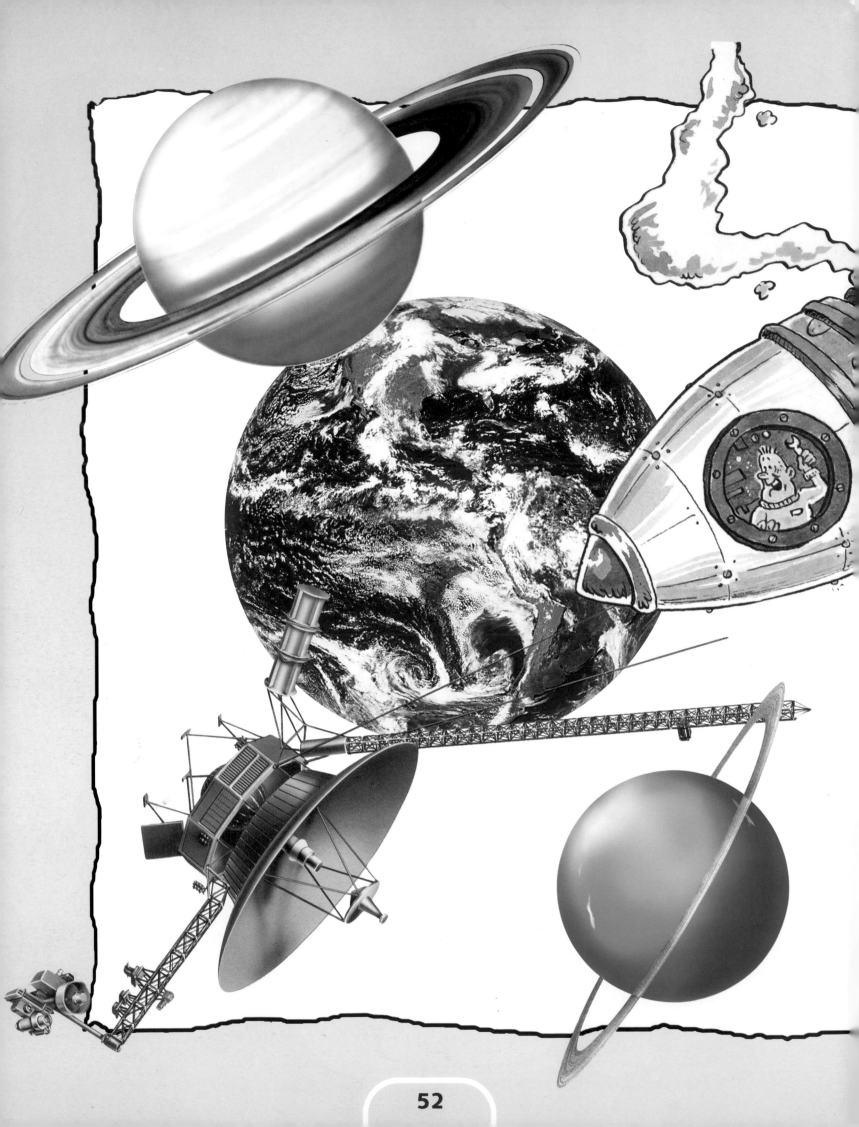

DEEP, DEEP SPACE

Our home, Earth, is just one of nine planets that travel around the Sun. And the Sun is an ordinary star, like billions of others in the vast Universe. Since ancient times people have studied the night sky to find out more about other galaxies and the vast empty space between them. In recent years we have sent people and telescopes into space, and this has taught us even more. Have fun finding out about astronomy and space travel, as well as how they might develop in the future.

PLANET EARTH

NEARLY THREE QUARTERS OF THE EARTH IS COVERED WITH OCEANS.

ocean

Our home, Earth, is a round planet that travels around the Sun in a part of the Universe called the Milky Way. A blanket of air is wrapped around the Earth, and this atmosphere allows humans, animals and plants to breathe and live. Looked at from space, our planet looks blue and white. The blue comes from the water which covers much of the Earth's surface, and the white patches are masses of clouds.

Earth has many special features, such as forests, mountains, deserts and oceans.

Factfile

- Earth's diameter is 12,756 km.

- Earth's circumference at the equator is 40,074 km.

- The Sahara is the biggest desert, stretching over 5,000 km from the Atlantic Ocean to the Red Sea.

- The Pacific is the biggest and deepest ocean; it covers more than a third of the Earth's surface.

mountains

- The highest mountain range is the Himalayas, in Asia; the longest is the Andes, in South America.

forest

desert

Earth on your window

1. Copy our blue and white planet Earth on your window. Powder paint mixed with water and washing-up liquid gives the most intense colours.

2. Paint on the inside of the window, so the rain can't ruin your artwork.

3. Tape newspaper to the bottom of the window to protect the window sill and floor.

4. You can wash the Earth off with a sponge and soapy water when you've grown tired of it or want to change planets.

MOON

Planet Earth has a satellite which circles around it as it travels through space. Satellites such as this are called moons, and we call ours simply the Moon. It is about a quarter the size of Earth, but it has no water and no air. Because it has no atmosphere and no weather, the Moon also has no life and it hardly changes. Its surface is covered with rocks and dust, as well as circular hollows called craters.

From Earth, the Moon appears to change shape because we see different parts of it lit by sunlight.

The Moon's diameter is just over a quarter the size of its mother planet, Earth.

new Moon

Factfile

- The Moon is 384,000 km from Earth; you would have to go around the Earth 9.5 times to travel this far.

- The Moon spins as it circles the Earth, so the same side always faces us.

- There are 29.5 days from one new Moon to the next.

- The Moon's craters were formed by chunks of space rock crashing into it.

WHAT'S ALL THIS ABOUT A 'SEA OF TRANQUILITY?'

Sea

Make a Moon calendar

1. Divide a large sheet of paper up into squares for the days of the month.

2. Each night, draw the shape of the Moon as you see it from your window. If the weather is clear, this will be easy. If there are a lot of clouds covering the Moon, just draw what you see that night.

3. Don't forget, when it's a new Moon, you won't see anything, so just draw a dark sky.

moon chart

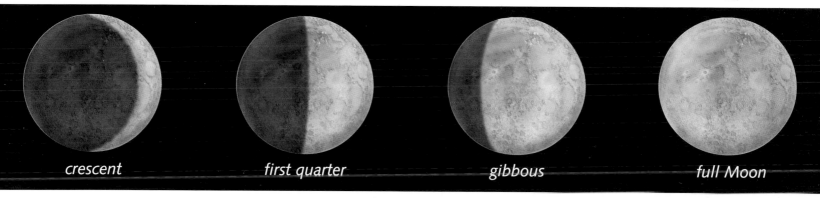

crescent   *first quarter*   *gibbous*   *full Moon*

Quiz

1 What do we call the phase of the Moon when we can't see it at all?
2 How many times have humans landed on the Moon?
3 How many times a month does the Moon circle the Earth?
4 What do we call the Moon's vast dry plains?
5 Is the Moon made of cheese?
6 What is an "earthquake" on the Moon called?

DID SOMEBODY SAY CHEESE?

Answers
1 New Moon. 2 Six. 3 Once.
4 Seas (because people once thought they were water).
5 No (only in fairy tales!). 6 Moonquake.

SOLAR SYSTEM

Our Earth is one of nine planets that travel around the Sun. Along with many moons, lumps of rock and comets, the Sun and its orbiting planets make up the solar system (solar means "to do with the Sun"). Everything in the solar system is connected to the Sun, at its centre, by an invisible force called gravity.

I CAN'T TALK RIGHT NOW DEAR, I'M AT WORK!

Quiz

1 Which is the second biggest planet?

2 How many planets have people walked on?

3 Which planet is smaller than our Moon?

4 What colour does Earth look from space?

5 Which two planets do not have moons?

6 Which planet was named after the Roman god of the sea?

Earth

Venus

Mercury

Answers
1 Saturn. 2 One – Earth. 3 Pluto.
4 Blue. 5 Mercury and Venus.
6 Neptune.

Factfile

- The largest planet, Jupiter, is big enough to hold over 1,300 Earths.
- The planet closest to the Sun, Mercury, travels around the Sun six times in one of our Earth years.
- The four giant outer planets – Jupiter, Saturn, Uranus and Neptune – are made of gas around a rocky core.
- Pluto is over a hundred times further away from the Sun than Mercury is.
- There are thousands of miniature planets, called asteroids, in the space between Mars and Jupiter.

Pluto

Neptune

Uranus

Saturn

GOOD JOB I REMEMBERED MY SPACE MAP!

Mars

Jupiter

Plasticine planets

1. You can mould plasticine around small round objects – beads, marbles, ping-pong balls – to make planets. Follow the colours on these pages for each one.
2. Mould a big yellow Sun around a larger ball.
3. Then put the planets in order on a black paper space background.

SUN

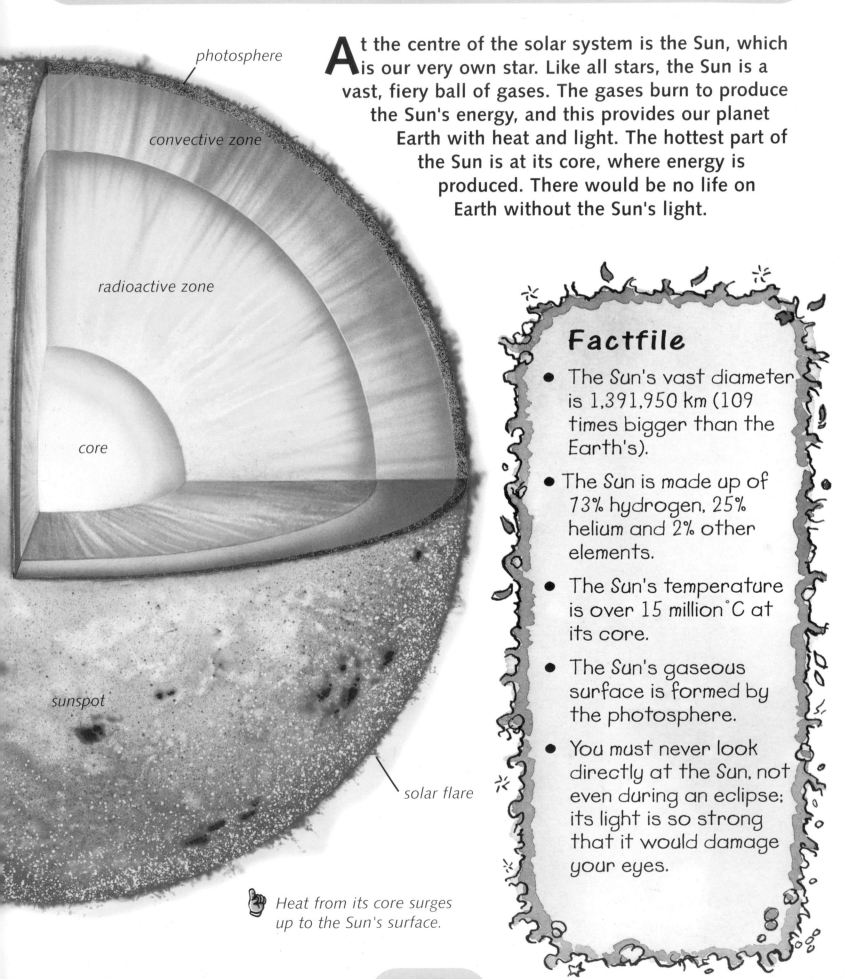

At the centre of the solar system is the Sun, which is our very own star. Like all stars, the Sun is a vast, fiery ball of gases. The gases burn to produce the Sun's energy, and this provides our planet Earth with heat and light. The hottest part of the Sun is at its core, where energy is produced. There would be no life on Earth without the Sun's light.

photosphere

convective zone

radioactive zone

core

sunspot

solar flare

☞ Heat from its core surges up to the Sun's surface.

Factfile

- The Sun's vast diameter is 1,391,950 km (109 times bigger than the Earth's).

- The Sun is made up of 73% hydrogen, 25% helium and 2% other elements.

- The Sun's temperature is over 15 million°C at its core.

- The Sun's gaseous surface is formed by the photosphere.

- You must never look directly at the Sun, not even during an eclipse; its light is so strong that it would damage your eyes.

 Sometimes the Moon is in the exact position to block out the Sun for a few minutes. This is called a solar eclipse.

Make a sundial clock

1. Push the blunt end of a pencil into plasticine and stand it on a piece of white card.

2. Starting in the morning on a sunny day, use a ruler and pen to mark where the shadow of the pencil falls every hour. Write the time next to the line (10 o'clock, 11 o'clock, and so on).

3. On the next sunny day, you can use your sundial clock to tell the time (remember, the card must remain in exactly the same spot).

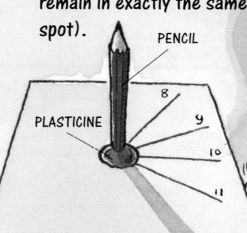

PENCIL

PLASTICINE

8
9
10
11

AHH... THIS IS THE LIFE!

Quiz

1 How many Earths would it take to make a ball as large as the Sun – more than a hundred, a thousand or a million?

2 What are small, dark patches on the Sun called?

3 The Earth is not always exactly the same distance from the Sun – true or false?

4 How long does it take for the Sun's rays to reach Earth – eight seconds, eight minutes or eight hours?

5 Is the Sun the biggest star?

6 How long does it take for the Earth to travel around the Sun?

Answers
1 More than a million.
2 Sunspots. 3 True. 4 Eight minutes. 5 No. 6 A year.

THE SUN IS HOTTEST ON THE PLANETS NEAREST TO IT, AND COOLER ON THOSE FURTHER AWAY!

DAYS AND SEASONS

The Earth is constantly spinning, like a top. At any one time, about half of the planet is facing the Sun, and this half is in daylight. As that half turns away from the Sun because of the Earth's spin, it gets dark and has night-time.

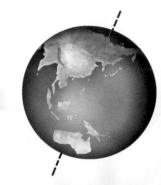

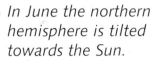 In June the northern hemisphere is tilted towards the Sun.

PHEW!

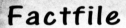

Factfile

- In the tropics, the hottest parts of the Earth near the Equator, it is warm all year round.

- Many trees drop their leaves in the autumn; this helps them survive the cold, dark winter.

- Twice during the year day and night are the same length of 12 hours each; the two equinoxes are on 21 March and 23 September.

- In the northern hemisphere, the longest day is around 21 June, and the shortest day around 21 December.

In September the northern 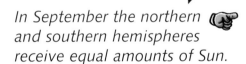 and southern hemispheres receive equal amounts of Sun.

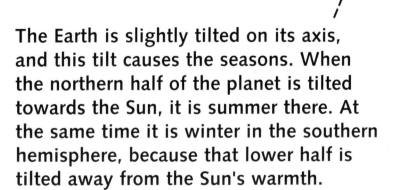

The Earth is slightly tilted on its axis, and this tilt causes the seasons. When the northern half of the planet is tilted towards the Sun, it is summer there. At the same time it is winter in the southern hemisphere, because that lower half is tilted away from the Sun's warmth.

The Earth spins right round once every 24 hours.

In June the northern half of the Earth is tilted towards the Sun. In December it is the exact opposite.

1 How many times does the Earth spin round in a year?

2 When it's summer in Europe, what season is it in Australia?

3 Which season comes after winter?

4 What is the southern half of the Earth called?

5 What is the northern tropic called?

6 When it's spring in London, what season is it in New York?

Answers
1 365 times. 2 Winter. 3 Spring.
4 Southern hemisphere.
5 Tropic of Cancer. 6 Spring.

👉 *In March the northern and southern hemispheres receive equal amounts of Sun.*

In December the 👉 *southern hemisphere is tilted towards the Sun.*

STOP THE WORLD, I WANT TO GET OFF

Day and night

1. For this activity, you need a globe of the Earth. If you haven't got one, use a plastic football and pretend. Your globe/ball is the Earth, and for the Sun you will need a torch.

2. In a darkened room, shine the torch at your globe. The side facing the torch (or Sun) is lit up, so there it is day. On the dark side of the globe it is night.

3. If you slowly spin the globe round, you will see how daylight moves around the Earth.

STARS

The night sky is full of stars. In fact, the day sky is full of them too, but the light from our local star, the Sun, blots them out. Each of the stars is a huge ball of gas that gives off vast amounts of light and heat. There are millions upon millions of stars in the universe. Some of them are so far away from Earth that it has taken millions of years for their light to reach us. When a star has used up all its energy, it stops shining and dies.

A nebula is a glowing cloud of dust and gas.

BEWARE BLACK HOLES!

TUG TUG

A star burns from a nuclear reaction inside it.

A red supergiant is an enormous star, 500 times the diameter of our Sun.

Quiz

1 Are some stars smaller than our Sun?

2 Some stars that we see in the night sky may no longer exist – true or false?

3 Have humans ever travelled to another star?

4 What is another name for the North Star?

5 Will our star, the Sun, ever die?

6 What are binary stars?

Answers

1 Yes. 2 True. 3 No. 4 Pole Star, or Polaris. 5 Yes (in about 5000 million years time). 6 Two stars that orbit each other.

Factfile

- Some stars are brighter than others; but a dim star that is close to our solar system can appear brighter than a more distant, brighter star.

- Astronomers measure in light years, which is the distance travelled by light in a year (equivalent to 9.46 million million km).

- The nearest star to our solar system is Proxima Centauri, which is 4.2 light years away.

- The brightest star in the night sky is Sirius, the dog-star.

Star mural

1. Let the stars twinkle on your wall. Cut out star shapes from shiny sweet wrappers. Use gold and silver foil for very bright stars. Stick the stars on a large sheet of black paper.

2. Brush some PVA glue onto the background and sprinkle on some glitter for a sparkling Milky Way. Shake off any unwanted glitter.

3. Then stick your star mural up on the wall with multi-purpose tac.

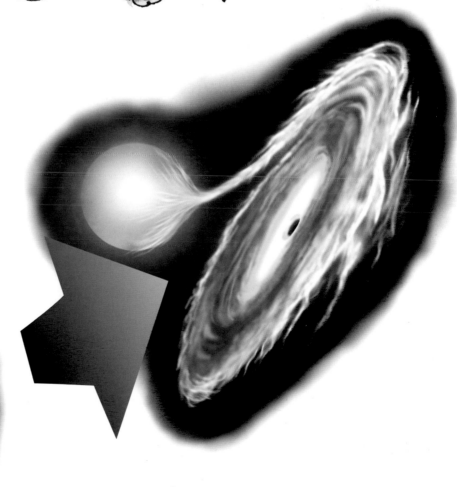

Some stars explode and produce a supernova.

The material left collapses in on itself. The gravity around that spot is so strong that not even light can escape, which is why it is called a black hole.

GALAXIES

Stars cluster together in groups called galaxies. These clusters have different shapes. Some are round, ball shapes, while others are completely irregular. All galaxies are spinning in space, and the shape of a galaxy depends on how fast it spins.

The Sun is just one of millions of stars in our galaxy, which is called the Milky Way. Ours is a spiral galaxy, and it got its name because from Earth it looks like a creamy band of stars across the sky.

Our star, the Sun, is on a spiral arm of the Milky Way galaxy.

This spiral galaxy is very similar in appearance to our own Milky Way.

Quiz

1 The word "galaxy" comes from an Ancient Greek term meaning what?

2 What is the constellation that looks like fishes called?

3 How long does it take light to travel right across the Milky Way?

4 The constellation of Libra is not an animal or a person, but what?

5 Is the Sun at the centre of the Milky Way galaxy?

6 How many constellations make up the signs of the zodiac?

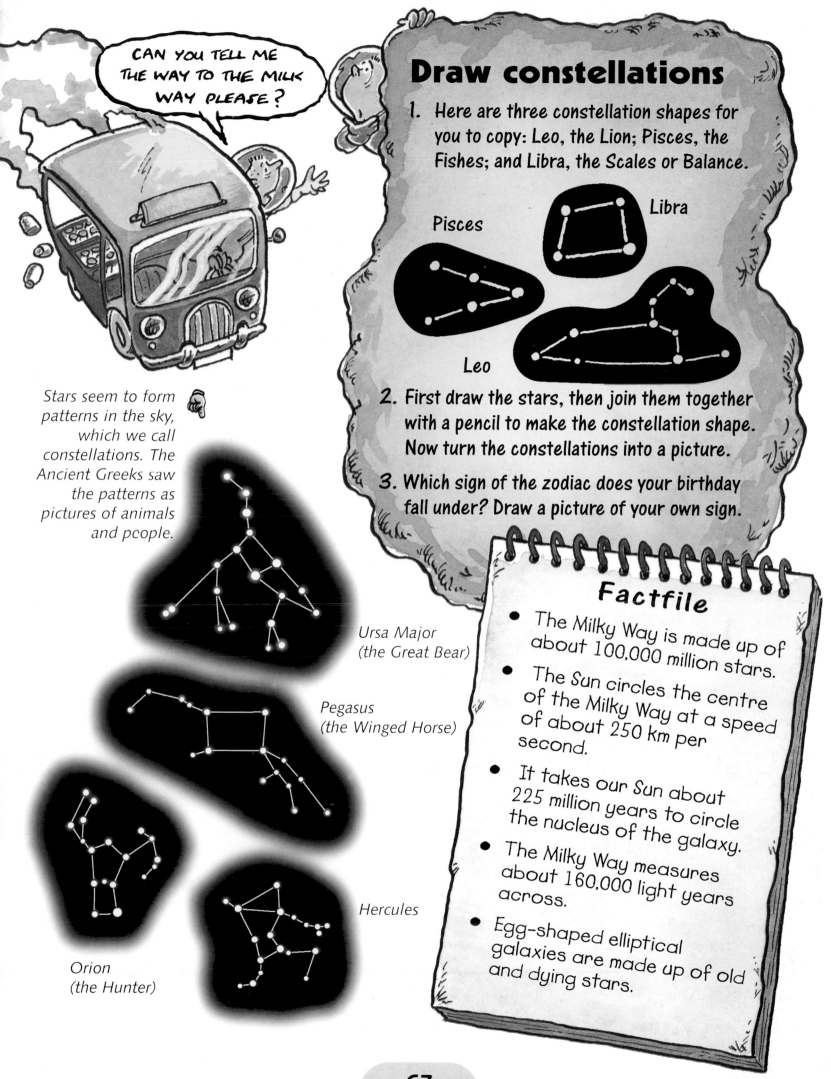

CAN YOU TELL ME THE WAY TO THE MILK WAY PLEASE?

Stars seem to form patterns in the sky, which we call constellations. The Ancient Greeks saw the patterns as pictures of animals and people.

Ursa Major
(the Great Bear)

Pegasus
(the Winged Horse)

Hercules

Orion
(the Hunter)

Draw constellations

1. Here are three constellation shapes for you to copy: Leo, the Lion; Pisces, the Fishes; and Libra, the Scales or Balance.

Pisces

Libra

Leo

2. First draw the stars, then join them together with a pencil to make the constellation shape. Now turn the constellations into a picture.

3. Which sign of the zodiac does your birthday fall under? Draw a picture of your own sign.

Factfile

- The Milky Way is made up of about 100,000 million stars.

- The Sun circles the centre of the Milky Way at a speed of about 250 km per second.

- It takes our Sun about 225 million years to circle the nucleus of the galaxy.

- The Milky Way measures about 160,000 light years across.

- Egg-shaped elliptical galaxies are made up of old and dying stars.

UNIVERSE

The Universe is the whole of space. It is the biggest thing there is, including all the stars, galaxies and the empty parts of space between them. We can only see a very small part of the Universe, even with the most powerful telescope.

Most scientists think that the Universe began with a Big Bang, about 15,000 million years ago. Since then it has been growing bigger and bigger in all directions, creating more and more space. The Universe is still expanding today.

Factfile

- Scientists think that before the Big Bang, all the material that existed was in one small lump.

- The Milky Way is in a cluster of about 30 galaxies called the Local Group (that could be added to Josie Bloggs' address too! – see below)

- In the 2nd century AD, the Egyptian astronomer Ptolemy stated that the Earth was at the centre of the Universe, with the Sun, Moon and five known planets orbiting around it.

- The most distant things that we have seen in the Universe are star-like objects that we call quasars.

☞ The Big Bang was a massive explosion that created the Universe.

Millions of ☞ years later, gases clustered into clouds.

IS THIS ADDRESS CLEAR ENOUGH?

Josie Bloggs
8 Acacia Avenue
Surbiton, Surrey
England
Europe
Earth
Solar System
Milky Way
Universe

☞ The clouds clumped together to form galaxies.

Quiz

1. Which is older, the Earth or the Universe?

2. What is the overall temperature of the Universe – 10°C, 0°C or –270°C?

3. Are galaxies moving closer together or further apart?

4. Is Andromeda a planet, a star or a galaxy?

5. Which galaxy and constellation are named after a lion?

6. When the Universe was very young, it contained just hydrogen and oxygen – true or false?

Answers
1 Universe. 2 –270°C.
3 Further apart. 4 Galaxy.
5 Leo. 6 False (it was hydrogen and helium).

We can see millions of stars in the night sky, but these are still just a tiny part of the Universe.

Expanding the Universe

1. Paint white, squiggly galaxies on a big blue or black balloon.

2. Let the paint dry, and then slowly blow up the balloon. As air fills it, you will see the galaxies moving apart, just as they are really doing in the Universe. If you stand in front of a mirror, you can see this more clearly.

MERCURY AND VENUS

Mercury

Venus

Mercury is the closest of the solar system's nine planets to the Sun. It is a small, rocky planet, which looks a bit like our Moon and is not much larger. The side of Mercury facing the Sun gets blisteringly hot – more than 420°C – because it is so close. The other side, however, is freezing cold – about -180°C.

The next planet out from the Sun, Venus, is slightly smaller than Earth. It has a thick atmosphere of carbon dioxide gas, which traps the Sun's heat and makes it even hotter than on Mercury.

Factfile

- Diameter: Mercury 4,878 km; Venus 12,104 km.

- Distance from the Sun: Mercury 58 million km; Venus 108 million km.

- Spin time in Earth days: Mercury 59; Venus 243.

- Orbit time around the Sun in Earth days: Mercury 88; Venus 225.

- Moons: neither planet has any moons.

- Venus' atmosphere pushes down with a pressure more than 90 times stronger than air pressure on Earth.

Mercury's surface has many small craters, like our Moon.

The surface of Venus has plains, craters, mountains and volcanoes.

> MY VERY EARLY MORNING JAM SANDWICH USUALLY NAUSEATES PEOPLE! THAT'S HOW I REMEMBER THE ORDER OF THE PLANETS, MERCURY, VENUS, EARTH...

Quiz

1. The Sun and planets were formed from a cloud of dust and what?

2. Venus is almost twice as far from the Sun as Mercury - true or false?

3. Are Mercury and Venus called inner or outer planets?

4. Which planet has the shortest day – Earth, Mercury or Venus?

5. Which planet was named after the Roman goddess of love?

6. Could humans breathe on Mercury or Venus?

Answers
1 Gas. 2 True. 3 Inner planets.
4 Earth. 5 Venus. 6 No.

COOKING OIL

WATER

FLOUR

Crater baking

1. To bake your own Mercurial craters, mix 250 g plain flour with 125 g salt and two spoonfuls of cooking oil. Mix in a little water until you have a non-sticky mixture.

2. Mould the dough to make a Mercuryscape, and use a fork and spoon to create craters.

3. Ask an adult for help. Line a baking sheet with foil and bake Mercury at the bottom of the oven for about 30 minutes at 180° centigrade or gas mark four. When it has cooled, put it on a cardboard base and paint the craters grey and black.

MARS

Mars is sometimes called the red planet, because its rocks and soil are a reddish colour. This is caused by iron oxide, the chemical name for rust. There is no running water on Mars, but dried-up river beds show that Mars did have water millions of years ago. The Viking spacecraft landed on the planet in 1976, and in 1997 the Pathfinder spacecraft sent the Sojourner rover vehicle to study the rocks on Mars and photograph them.

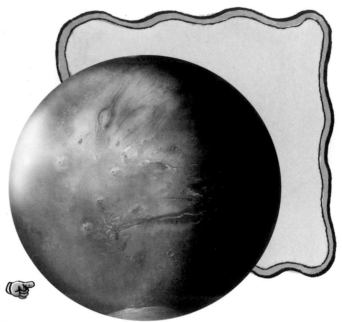

The surface of  Mars shows signs of volcanic activity.

 The six-wheeled, remote-controlled rover named Sojourner was specially designed to move about on Mars.

Factfile

- Diameter: 6,787 km.

- Distance from the Sun: 228 million km.

- Spin time in Earth days: one (24 hours and 37 minutes).

- Orbit time around the Sun in Earth days: 687.

- Moons: two; the irregular-shaped Deimos is 12 km across and is the smallest moon in the solar system; Mars' other moon, Phobos, is a bit larger.

- Atmosphere: 95% carbon dioxide and 3% nitrogen, with traces of oxygen, argon, carbon monoxide and water.

Quiz

1 Mars was named after the Roman god of what?

2 How long did it take *Pathfinder* to fly to Mars from Earth – seven weeks, seven months or seven years?

3 Mars has two polar icecaps – true or false?

4 How many planets are there between Mars and Pluto?

5 Which has a longer day, Mars or Earth?

6 Which US spacecraft first flew close to Mars in 1965?

Answers

1 War 2 Seven months 3 True. 4 Four. 5 Mars. 6 Mariner.

Olympus Mons is the largest of Mars' four giant volcanoes. It is 600 km across at the base and 27 km high.

Marbled Mars

1. To make marbled Mars paper, put blobs of orange, red and brown oil paint on a plate.

2. With the help of an adult, mix a few drops of white spirit into it with a knife, to make the paint runny.

3. Use a bowl of water that is at least as big as your piece of paper. Plop the paint off the knife into the water and swirl it round gently. Alternatively, you can put drops of marbling ink straight into the water.

4. Place your paper on top of the floating colours for 30 seconds. Then lift it off, turn it over and hold it flat to stop the paint running.

5. When the paper is dry, you can use it as Martian gift-wrap.

THE HIGHEST POINT ON EARTH IS ONLY A THIRD AS HIGH AS OLYMPUS MONS

GRRRR!!

JUPITER

The largest planet in the solar system lies beyond a band of mini-planets called the asteroid belt. Jupiter is a gas giant, made mainly of hydrogen around a rock-iron core. The planet is so big that its core alone weighs about 15 times more than planet Earth.

It has large cloud features that swirl around its surface, as well as a system of rings that were only discovered in 1979.

Jupiter's four biggest moons are sometimes called the Galilean moons, because in 1610 the famous Italian astronomer Galileo discovered them.

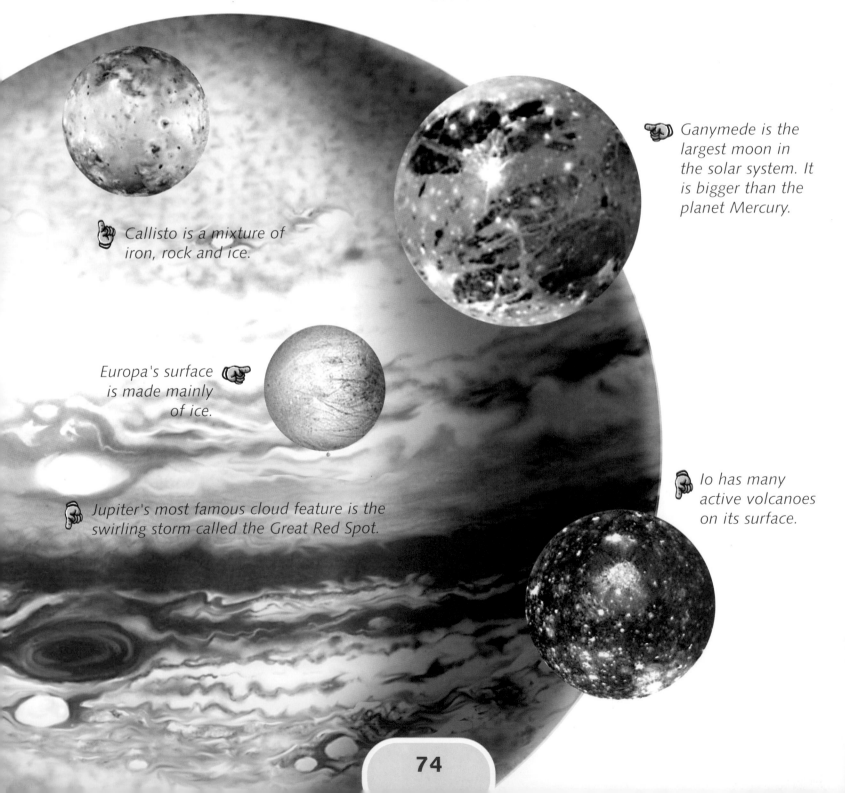

Ganymede is the largest moon in the solar system. It is bigger than the planet Mercury.

Callisto is a mixture of iron, rock and ice.

Europa's surface is made mainly of ice.

Jupiter's most famous cloud feature is the swirling storm called the Great Red Spot.

Io has many active volcanoes on its surface.

Factfile

- Diameter: 142,796 km.
- Distance from the Sun: 778 million km.
- Spin time in Earth hours: ten.
- Jupiter's rings have three parts: an inner halo, a bright central ring, and an outer thin ring which extends out to 214,000 km.
- Moons: 16, including the four Galilean moons.
- Orbit time around the Sun in Earth years: 11.9.

I'M JUPITER, KING OF THE ROMAN GODS; THIS PLANET WAS NAMED AFTER ME.

Zoom off to Jupiter

1. Everyone who plays this game is on the way to Jupiter, but who will get there first?

2. Copy the board on a large piece of card. Starting at square one, move your counter according to the number you throw on a dice.

3. Every time you land on a square with the bottom of a rocket, zoom to the top. When you land on the tail of a comet, you must slide right down to the head. When you land on a lost-in-space square, you miss a turn. You might be lucky and meet a friendly alien who'll show you a short cut to Jupiter.

SATURN

The second largest planet, Saturn, is most famous for its beautiful system of rings. It is a bit smaller than Jupiter, and in many ways is quite similar. It is made mainly of hydrogen and helium, around a hot solid core, and the temperature above the clouds on its surface is -178°C.

The seven main rings of Saturn are made up of thousands of ringlets. The main ring system is more than 270,000 km across, but only about 10 m thick. The rings are made of tiny ice particles.

Saturn's most famous feature is its system of rings. Saturn's largest moon, Titan, has an atmosphere made mainly of nitrogen.

DID YOU KNOW THAT SATURN WAS THE ROMAN GOD OF FARMING AND THE FATHER OF JUPITER?

Factfile

- Diameter: 120,000 km.

- Distance from the Sun: 1,424 million km.

- Spin time in Earth hours: 10.5.

- Orbit time around the Sun in Earth years: 29.5.

- Moons: 18 have been identified, but there may be more.

- The third largest moon, Iapetus, has black deposits on its surface; this may be dust from a comet impact on another nearby moon.

Quiz

1 How many complete orbits of the Sun does Earth make while Saturn makes one?

2 Titan is the only moon in the solar system with a real atmosphere – true or false?

3 How many times does Saturn spin around in an Earth day?

4 What is the basic colour of Saturn – blue, green or yellow?

5 Is Saturn visible from Earth without a telescope?

6 Which day of the week comes from the god Saturn?

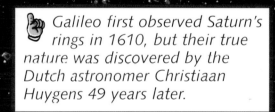

☝ Galileo first observed Saturn's rings in 1610, but their true nature was discovered by the Dutch astronomer Christiaan Huygens 49 years later.

Hang up Saturn

1. Screw some newspaper into a ball (about 15 cm in diameter) and secure it with masking tape.

2. Tear newspaper into small strips. Mix some PVA glue and water into a paste and dip the strips in. Cover the ball evenly.

3. Now cover the ball with white paper strips and leave the model to dry. Then paint it yellow.

4. Draw a 17 cm wide circle on card. Then draw a 20 cm circle around it. Cut out the inner circle, then cut around the outer line and paint rings of colour on your card circle.

5. Attach the ring to Saturn with card tabs. Stick the tabs to the ring, fold them and tape them to the planet, leaving a small gap all around.

6. Tape nylon thread to Saturn and hang it from the ceiling.

BALL OF NEWSPAPER

WHITE PAPER STRIPS

PAPER RING

CARD TABS

URANUS, NEPTUNE AND PLUTO

Uranus was the first planet discovered since ancient times. British astronomer William Herschel identified it in 1781. It is a large gas planet, and its surface is covered with blue-green clouds of tiny methane crystals. In 1986, Voyager 2 passed near Uranus and photographed its rings and some new moons. Three years later, Voyager 2 reached Neptune and once again found rings and more moons. Pluto is a small, frozen planet with a temperature of about -230°C.

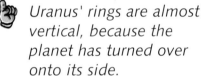

Neptune was discovered in 1846 by the German astronomer Johann Gottfried Galle.

Uranus' rings are almost vertical, because the planet has turned over onto its side.

Pluto is the smallest planet in our Solar System, and the furthest from the Sun.

Factfile

- Diameter: Uranus 51,118 km; Neptune 49,532 km; Pluto 2,320 km.

- Distance from the Sun: Uranus 2,866 million km; Neptune 4,488 million km; Pluto 5,906 million km.

- Spin time in Earth hours: Uranus 17; Neptune 16; Pluto 154 (over six days).

- Orbit time around the Sun in Earth years: Uranus 84; Neptune 165; Pluto 248.

- Moons: Uranus 15; Neptune eight; Pluto one

- Pluto's single moon, Charon, is about half its size; its surface is covered in ice.

Planets and gods

Which planet is named after which god?
Follow the jumbled lines with your finger to find out.

God of the heavens

God of the sea

Pluto

Neptune

Uranus

God of the underworld

Astronomers learned a great deal about Neptune from the spacecraft *Voyager 2*, which is now still continuing its journey beyond the solar system.

WHAT A WEIRD-LOOKING CRAFT!

Quiz

1 Which two planets cannot be seen from Earth with the naked eye?

2 When was Pluto first discovered?

3 Is Pluto more than twice as far from the Sun as Uranus?

4 Is Uranus' axis nearly vertical or horizontal?

5 Neptune's largest moon is called Kryton – true or false?

6 When was *Voyager 2* launched from Earth – 1970, 1977 or 1984?

Answers

1 Neptune and Pluto. 2 1930. 3 Yes. 4 Horizontal. 5 False (it's Triton). 6 1977.

COMETS AND METEORS

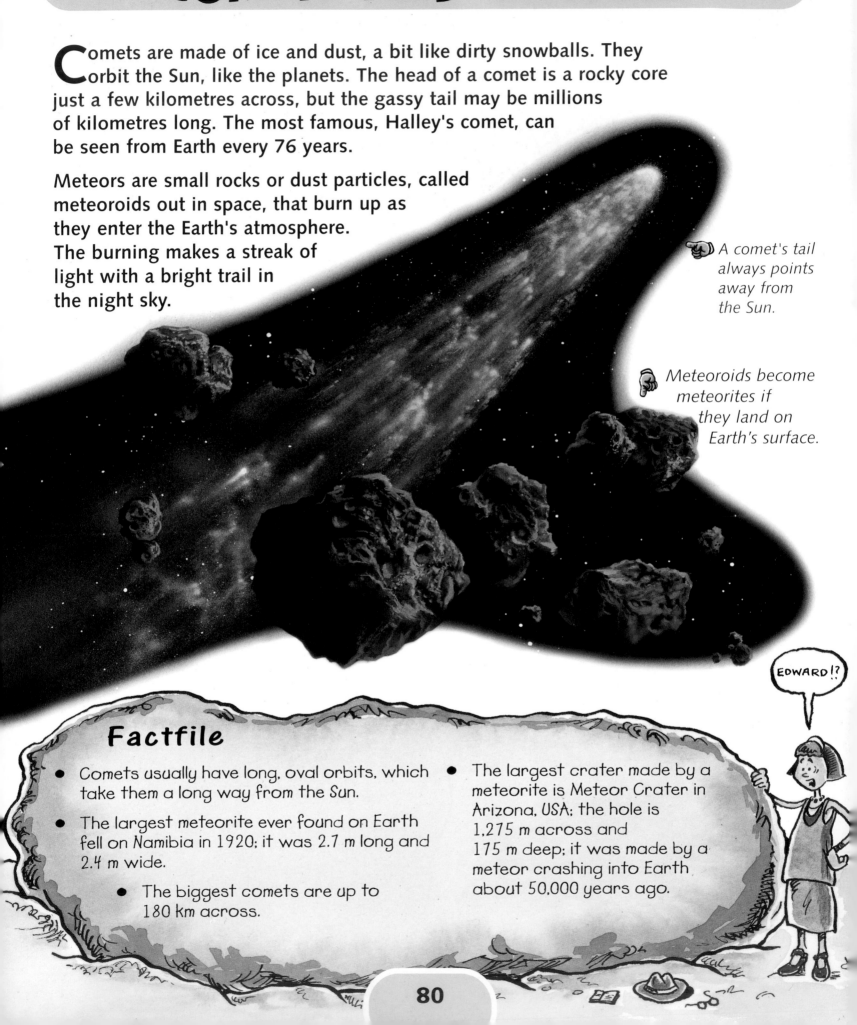

Comets are made of ice and dust, a bit like dirty snowballs. They orbit the Sun, like the planets. The head of a comet is a rocky core just a few kilometres across, but the gassy tail may be millions of kilometres long. The most famous, Halley's comet, can be seen from Earth every 76 years.

Meteors are small rocks or dust particles, called meteoroids out in space, that burn up as they enter the Earth's atmosphere. The burning makes a streak of light with a bright trail in the night sky.

A comet's tail always points away from the Sun.

Meteoroids become meteorites if they land on Earth's surface.

EDWARD!?

Factfile

- Comets usually have long, oval orbits, which take them a long way from the Sun.

- The largest meteorite ever found on Earth fell on Namibia in 1920; it was 2.7 m long and 2.4 m wide.

- The biggest comets are up to 180 km across.

- The largest crater made by a meteorite is Meteor Crater in Arizona, USA; the hole is 1,275 m across and 175 m deep; it was made by a meteor crashing into Earth about 50,000 years ago.

Pilot a spaceship

1. Join your spaceship at the bottom left of the picture.

2. Then, with your finger, try to pilot the spaceship on a safe flight path past all the meteoroids and comets, till you reach the other side.

HOME

Wooahhh!!!

Quiz

1 What is a shooting star?

2 Who are comets usually named after?

3 What is a meteor called out in space?

4 What is a meteor called on the Earth's surface?

5 Which comet appeared in the Bayeux Tapestry?

6 Can you see comets with the naked eye?

Answers
1 A meteorite. 2 The person who first discovers them. 3 Meteoroid. 4 Meteorite. 5 Halley's comet 6 Yes.

TRAVELLING IN SPACE

The first person to travel in space was a Russian, Yuri Gagarin, who circled the Earth once in 1961. A few weeks later the Americans sent their first astronaut into space – for just 15 minutes. Eight years later space travel had developed so much that a man was standing on the surface of the Moon. Since then astronauts have learned to live in space for longer periods and have conducted many useful experiments. There are even plans to send astronauts to Mars in the future.

FRANK, I THINK YOU'VE FORGOTTEN SOMETHING!

An astronaut can move freely through space on a special Manned Manoeuvring Unit, or MMU, which is guided by small jets.

Factfile

- In space there is so little gravity that everything floats, including astronauts and their food.

- The first living thing to travel in space was a dog called Laika, in 1957.

- There were five more successful Moon landings after *Apollo 11* in 1969.

- The first woman in space was Russian Valentina Tereshkova in 1963.

- On the last Apollo mission to the Moon, astronauts spent 76 hours on the lunar surface.

Make a moonscape

1. Mix four cups of plain flour and one cup of salt in a bowl. Add some yellow food colouring to a mug of water. Stir in as much water as needed, a little at a time, and knead it into a non-sticky mixture.

2. Shape the dough into a lunar surface with mountains and craters. You could even make some astronauts' footprints.

3. To make a lunar module, cover an eggbox cup with silver foil and stick a toothpaste lid on top. Shorten four bendy straws and glue them to the cup. Each leg is held with plasticine in a toothpaste-lid foot.

 Neil Armstrong was the first human to set foot on the Moon when he left his lunar module, called Eagle.

Quiz

1 What was the four-wheeled vehicle that astronauts took to the Moon called ?

2 Who was the first American in space?

3 What is a Russian astronaut called?

4 Did all the astronauts who landed on the Moon get back to Earth safely?

5 Is there air inside a spacecraft?

6 Is there air on the Moon?

Answers
1 Lunar Rover. 2 Alan Shepard.
3 Cosmonaut 4 Yes.
5 Yes. 6 No.

ROCKETS

Spacecraft, astronauts and satellites are launched into space by huge rockets. These work in the same way as firework rockets, burning fuel to force hot gases out at the back and so push the rocket forwards. Powerful space rockets burn enormous amounts of fuel very quickly, and most have two or three stages, which are really separate rockets stacked on top of each other. All this energy is needed to escape the pull of Earth's gravity.

Rockets burn fuel very 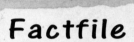 *rapidly to produce their power. A rocket can burn about two million litres of fuel in the first two and a half minutes of flight.*

ahhh!!!

Factfile

- Spacecraft need a speed of over 40,000 km/h (20 times faster than a Concorde plane) to escape Earth's gravity and get out into space.

- Gunpowder firework rockets were invented in Ancient China.

- The first space rocket was launched in Massachusetts, USA, in 1926, but it only reached a height of 12.5 m!

- Saturn V was 111 m tall and blasted off with the power equivalent to 160 jumbo jet engines.

Quiz

1 Rockets carry their own supply of oxygen, so that their fuel will burn in space – true or false?

2 At which space centre are American rockets launched?

3 In which country are Russian rockets launched?

4 What does NASA stand for?

5 In which American city was mission control for the Moon landings?

6 Ariane rockets are launched by ESA; what does ESA stand for?

Answers

1 True. 2 Kennedy Space Center. 3 Kazakhstan. 4 National Aeronautics and Space Administration. 5 Houston, Texas. 6 European Space Agency.

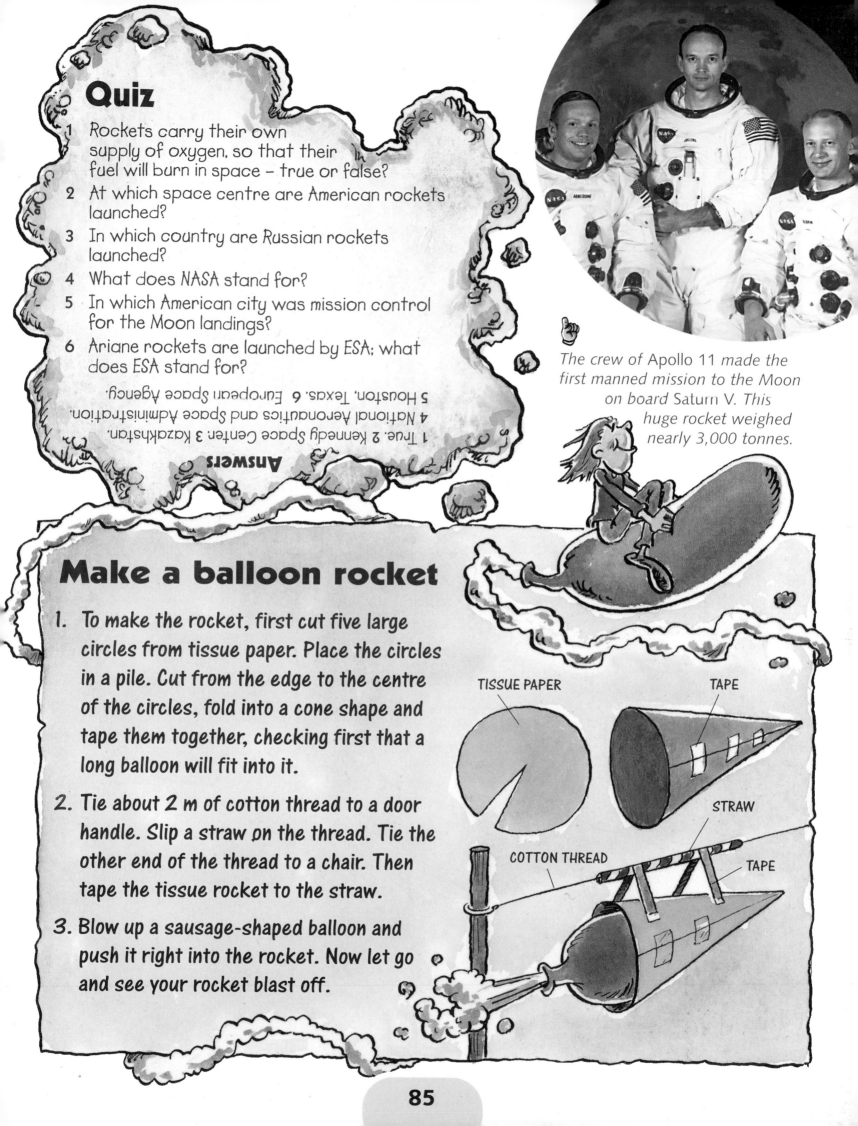

The crew of Apollo 11 *made the first manned mission to the Moon on board* Saturn V. *This huge rocket weighed nearly 3,000 tonnes.*

Make a balloon rocket

1. To make the rocket, first cut five large circles from tissue paper. Place the circles in a pile. Cut from the edge to the centre of the circles, fold into a cone shape and tape them together, checking first that a long balloon will fit into it.

2. Tie about 2 m of cotton thread to a door handle. Slip a straw on the thread. Tie the other end of the thread to a chair. Then tape the tissue rocket to the straw.

3. Blow up a sausage-shaped balloon and push it right into the rocket. Now let go and see your rocket blast off.

TISSUE PAPER

TAPE

STRAW

COTTON THREAD

TAPE

SHUTTLE

During the 1960s and 1970s space travel was extremely expensive because rockets and spacecraft were only ever used once. Then scientists invented the space shuttle, a reusable craft that can fly into space and land on Earth again many times. The American space shuttle Columbia was first launched in 1981, and since then shuttles have been used to take satellites into space, as well as taking astronauts to and from space stations.

 Then the empty fuel tank separates.

After launch, the two booster rockets fall away from the shuttle.

I'VE BOOKED TO GO ON THE FIRST SPACE SHUTTLE SERVICE FOR PAYING PASSENGERS.

The space shuttle is launched on the back of a huge fuel tank and two extra booster rockets.

Factfile

- An American space shuttle can carry up to seven astronauts, plus a cargo of satellites.

- The landing runway at Kennedy Space Center is 4,572 m long.

- In 1986 shuttle *Challenger* exploded after take-off and all seven astronauts were killed.

- A shuttle's main fuel tank is 47 m long.

- Space shuttles are taken to the launch pad on a crawler-transporter that moves on eight sets of caterpillar tracks at a top speed of 1.6 km/h.

The shuttle has its own jets to use in space.

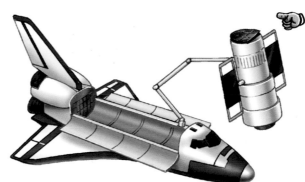

The shuttle is used to take satellites into space. It can also take astronauts to help fix satellites if they go wrong in orbit.

Quiz

1 How long is a US shuttle – 27 m, 37 m or 47 m?

2 Are the shuttle's booster rockets re-used?

3 What was the name of the fifth US shuttle, launched in 1992?

4 How many crew does the crawler-transporter have – 6, 16 or 26?

5 In which US state is Kennedy Space Center?

6 What is the shuttle's cargo hold called?

Answers
1 37 m. 2 Yes. 3 Endeavour.
4 26. 5 Florida. 6 Payload bay.

The shuttle glows red-hot when it re-enters the Earth's atmosphere.

The shuttle lands like a giant glider on a long runway.

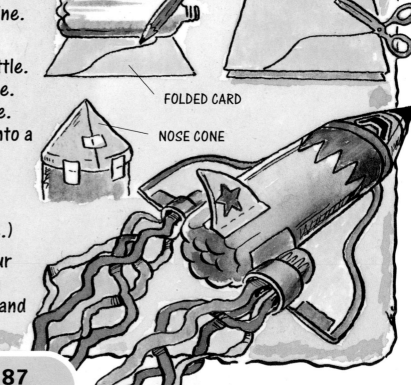

Make a space shuttle

1. Put a large plastic bottle on a piece of white card. Draw one shuttle wing, as shown. Fold the card in half and cut along the pencil line. Tape the wings to the bottle.

2. Cut out a tailpiece and tape it on the shuttle. Tape two yoghurt-pot engines at each side. Make a nose cone from a cardboard circle. Cut a segment out of the circle, form it into a cone and fit it around the bottle top.

3. Paint the shuttle white with acrylic paint. (Poster paint mixed with a few drops of washing-up liquid will also stick to plastic.)

4. When the white paint is dry, decorate your shuttle with stickers and silver foil. For a fiery exhaust, stick strips of red, yellow and pink paper inside the engines.

FOLDED CARD

NOSE CONE

SATELLITES AND PROBES

Hundreds of manmade space satellites are orbiting the Earth and sending back information all the time. Some send phone calls or television pictures around the world, while others help weather forecasters or help fix a position on Earth for sailors or even mountaineers.

Space probes have explored the planets, many of their moons, comets and other parts of space. They carry cameras and other equipment to give scientists close-up information that they simply could not gain from Earth.

Phone messages and TV pictures are sent up to telecommunications satellites, which bounce the information back to another part of the world.

Factfile

- Some satellites will stay in orbit around the Earth for hundreds or thousands of years; they will become space junk, along with old bits of rockets and other manmade material.

- In 1970, a year after *Apollo 11* landed on the Moon, an unmanned Luna craft brought Moon rock back to Earth, and a Lunokhod probe crawled over the lunar surface.

- The *International Violet Explorer* satellite was launched in 1978 and was expected to send back information for three years; to scientists' amazement, it went on working for 18 years.

HOUSTON, WE HAVE A PROBLEM!!

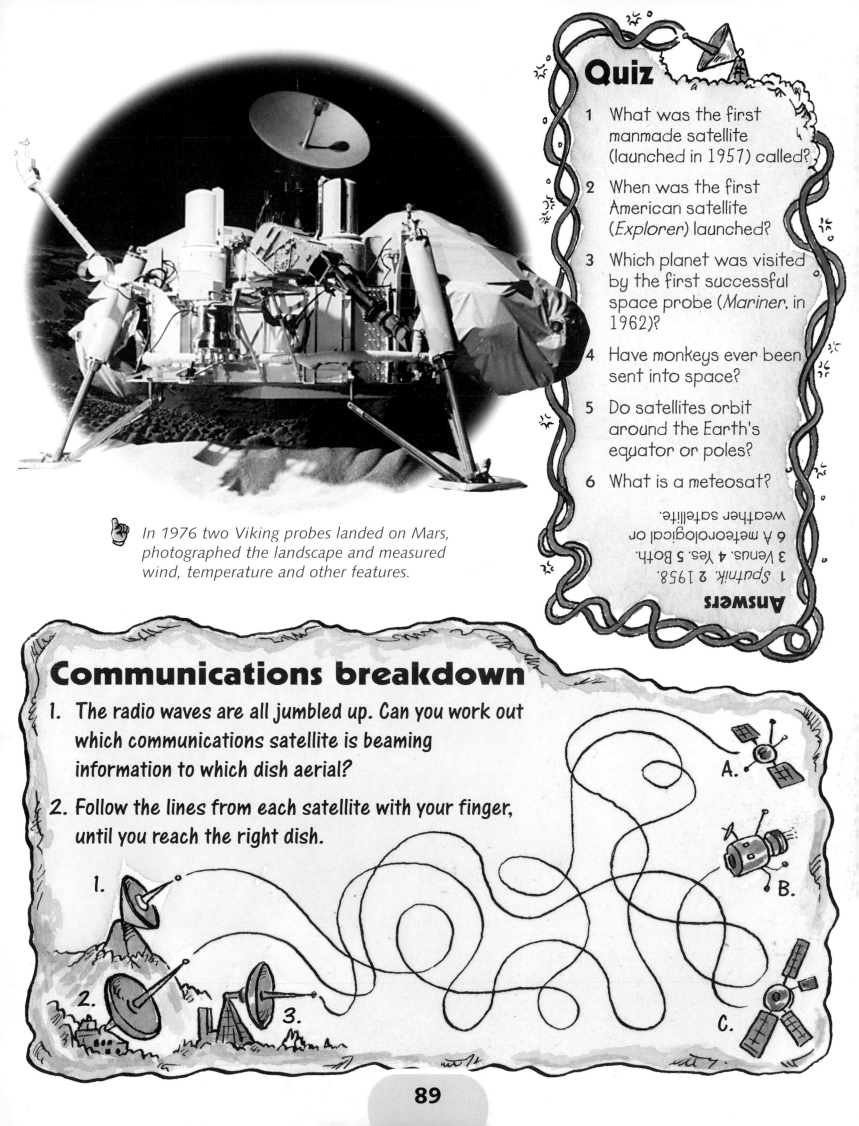

In 1976 two Viking probes landed on Mars, photographed the landscape and measured wind, temperature and other features.

Quiz

1 What was the first manmade satellite (launched in 1957) called?

2 When was the first American satellite (*Explorer*) launched?

3 Which planet was visited by the first successful space probe (*Mariner*, in 1962)?

4 Have monkeys ever been sent into space?

5 Do satellites orbit around the Earth's equator or poles?

6 What is a meteosat?

Answers
1 *Sputnik.* 2 1958.
3 Venus. 4 Yes. 5 Both.
6 A meteorological or weather satellite.

Communications breakdown

1. The radio waves are all jumbled up. Can you work out which communications satellite is beaming information to which dish aerial?

2. Follow the lines from each satellite with your finger, until you reach the right dish.

1.

2.

3.

A.

B.

C.

TELESCOPES

Astronomers use very powerful telescopes to see as far as possible out into the Universe. The telescopes have a mirror or lens to collect the light from an object. Big telescopes are protected inside domed buildings called observatories. The shape of the dome allows the telescope to rotate completely, giving astronomers a view of the entire night sky. In 1990 the Hubble space telescope was launched by a shuttle, and this has given even better views from space.

The Hubble space telescope was designed to see objects seven times further away than Earth-based telescopes.

Factfile

- Radio telescopes pick up and send radio signals. The world's largest radio telescope at Arecibo, in Puerto Rico has a 305 m dish.

- In December 1993, astronauts on shuttle *Endeavour* spent over 35 hours servicing and correcting faults on the Hubble space telescope – in space!

- The two Keck telescopes on Mauna Kea mountain, Hawaii, are the largest in the world. Each telescope has a 10 m mirror.

- The Very Large Telescope on top of a mountain in northern Chile is actually a group of four telescopes that work together.

Star-gazing

1. It's fun to star-gaze with friends and family. On a clear, dark night you can usually see hundreds of stars with the naked eye. If you use a pair of binoculars, you should be able to see thousands of stars – and much more clearly.

2. One way to identify stars and constellations is to use a planisphere, which is a star map that you can turn round and set to a specific time.

3. If you want to find out more or start using a telescope, you could join your local astronomical society.

WOW, THERE'S SOMEONE LOOKING BACK AT ME!!

Quiz

1 Which famous Italian scientist helped develop the telescope in 1609?

2 What was the first name of the US astronomer who gave his name to the space telescope?

3 Who designed the Royal Greenwich Observatory (in 1675)?

4 What does VLT stand for?

5 What are the two large panels on the sides of the space telescope designed to catch?

6 What is a scientist who studies space and the stars called?

Answers

1 Galileo. 2 Edwin (Hubble). 3 Sir Christopher Wren. 4 Very Large Telescope. 5 Solar energy. 6 An astronomer.

The best observatories are on mountain tops, well away from the bright lights of cities.

SPACE STATIONS

Space stations are large craft designed to stay in space for a long time and so act as a base for astronauts. The most successful so far has been the Russian Mir (meaning "Peace"), which was first launched in 1986 and had many further modules added later. It finally became so spacious that astronauts called it a "space hotel". By 1999 Mir's operations were finished and scientists from all over the world were working on a new international space station.

Space scientists from all over the world are working on a new international space station.

IT'S NOT SO EASY CHECKING INTO THE SPACE HOTEL!!

Factfile

- A Russian cosmonaut spent a record 437 days aboard the Mir space station.

- The 21 tonne, 13 m long base unit of Mir was lifted into orbit by a Proton rocket that was specially designed to carry heavy loads.

- Unmanned spacecraft are used to deliver supplies and take away rubbish from space stations.

- The first space station was the Russian Salyut, launched in 1971.

The Russian space station Mir started off as a small project, but grew as further modules were added and astronauts from other nations visited it.

Junk station

1. Mark a large piece of cardboard into three sections and stand it up. The panels are your control room. Fix various sizes of cardboard boxes and cartons along the top, bottom and sides with tape, and then paint them.

2. For the instrument panels use old metal scraps, nuts, bolts and lids; any old parts from broken radios, bikes, clocks and other machines could be useful too. Attach them to the boxes with strong glue.

3. For essential space equipment cover dishes, tubes and yoghurt pots with silver foil. Put up charts, graphs and space-age designs. Then get in touch with ground control!

LIFE IN SPACE!

Are there other forms of life in the Universe, apart from human beings, animals and plants on Earth? We don't know, but many scientists believe this is very likely. Some people claim to have seen strange spacecraft approaching Earth, but most of these "unidentified flying objects" have been explained or have proved to be hoaxes. Others claim to have seen aliens – beings from another world. Unmanned probes have found no signs of life on other planets in our Solar System. But Martian rocks found on Earth show that there may once have been microscopic forms of life on Mars.

Supposed alien spacecraft are sometimes called "flying saucers". They might look more like this one.

In many science fiction books and films, aliens are shown as unfriendly. But perhaps they would want to be friends with us.

Factfile

- For years scientists have been sending radio signals into space, hoping for a reply; they haven't had one yet.

- Astronomers have discovered planets orbiting stars outside our Solar System; perhaps there is life on one of those planets?

- There are millions of stars in our galaxy, and millions of galaxies in the Universe: isn't it likely that life exists on more than one small planet?

Playdough aliens

1. Get out the playdough – the more colours you can find the better– and make some alien friends.

2. There are no limits in space. Odd shaped creatures, long thin sausage aliens and round heads without bodies might all live in a galaxy far, far away.

3. You can add pipe-cleaners, buttons and other bits and pieces for that Extra-Terrestrial touch.

Quiz

1   What does UFO stand for?

2   What are the inhabitants of Earth called?

3   What does ET stand for?

4   Who made the Star Wars films?

5   What is the name of the doctor who time-travels in the Tardis?

6   Does alien life exist?

Answers

1 Unidentified Flying Object
2 Earthlings 3 Extra-Terrestrial.
4 George Lucas. 5 Dr Who.
6 Give your own answer – we don't know!

IT MUST BE SOME SORT OF WEIRD RITUAL, THEY WATCH IT ALL THE TIME!

INTO THE FUTURE

What will happen to the Universe in the future? Most scientists believe that it will go on expanding, until – many millions of years from now – the galaxies start to fall back towards the centre of the Universe and come together in a big crunch. Our star, the Sun, won't last that long, but will burn out in about 5,000 million years time.

In the near future, humans may find ways to visit other planets and even stars. Scientists are already working on a new mission, to send astronauts to Mars.

Mars is a very cold and windy planet. A Martian base for humans will need protective buildings with their own air supply.

Factfile

- The furthest humans have travelled is to the Moon. Mars is over 200 times further away.

- The fastest speed at which humans have ever travelled is around 40,000 km/h; light travels 27,000 times faster than this!

- If humans ever found a way to travel at the speed of light, which scientists think is the fastest speed possible in the Universe, it would still take over four years to reach the next nearest star to the Sun.

- Some scientists think that a future Big Crunch might be followed by another Big Bang – all in millions and millions of years time.

WELL, IT SAYS IT'S HOT IN THE BROCHURE

In future, faster space planes may take over from shuttles, so that humans can visit other planets.

Foil space city

1. Collect plastic packaging, cardboard tubes, egg cartons, plastic bottles, yoghurt pots, cans, lids, tops and foil dishes.

2. You need the base of a large cardboard box to build your space city on. Study your collection first and decide on a layout for the city before glueing everything down.

3. Cover all the items with foil. Plastic bottles cut in half make domes for Earthlings to live in. Tubes and cans make a network of passages connecting buildings and towers. Satellite dishes can be made from lids and foil.

4. Stick everything to the cardboard base, then paint the base white. Wait for it to dry before moving into foil city.

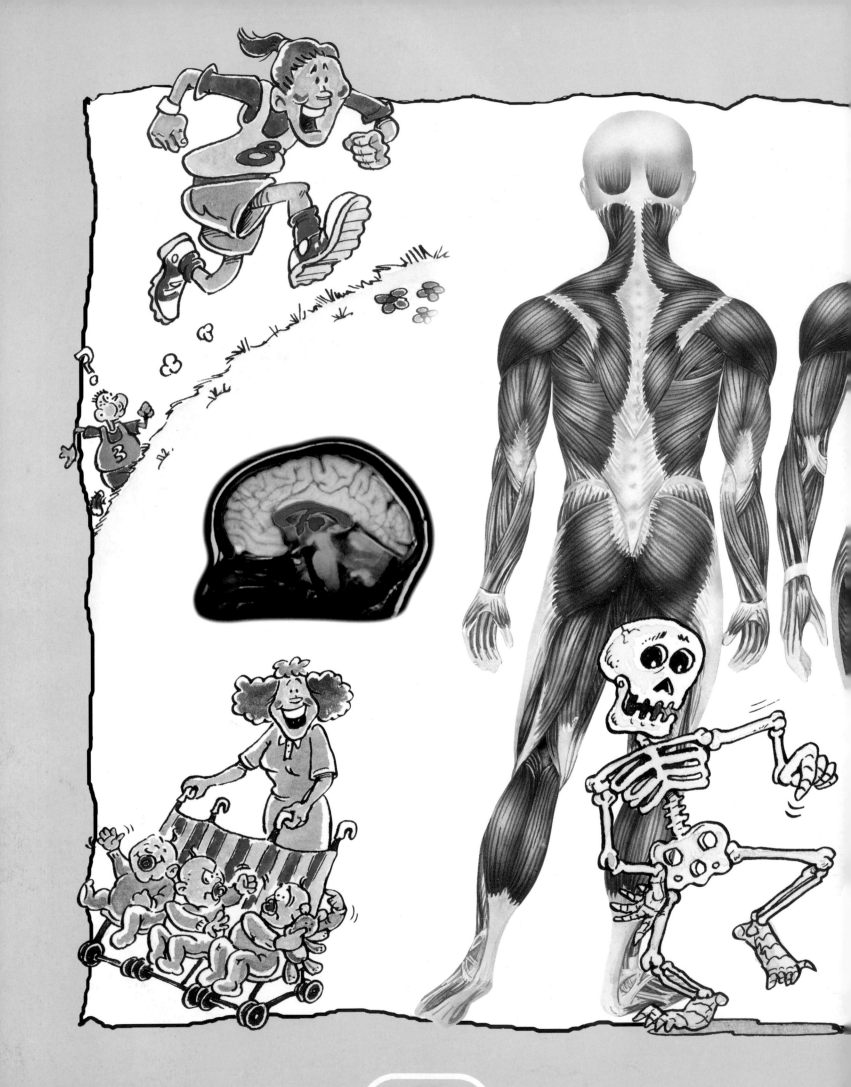

YOUR INCREDIBLE BODY

The human body is made up of many different parts, all working together to help keep us alive and healthy. There are lots of fascinating facts to learn about ourselves and our hard-working bodies, from the powerful muscles that make us move to the millions of tiny brain cells that make up our control centre.

The body's parts may look and work the same way in all of us, yet we are all different from each other. Have fun finding out about your unique and amazing body.

PARTS OF THE BODY

The human body is made up of many different parts, each with its own special job to do. All these parts, from the tiniest cells throughout our body to the biggest bones in our legs, are alive. They all need energy to make them work, which they get from the food we eat. And they all work together to make us a whole person. Though our bodies may all be similar, no two people are exactly the same.

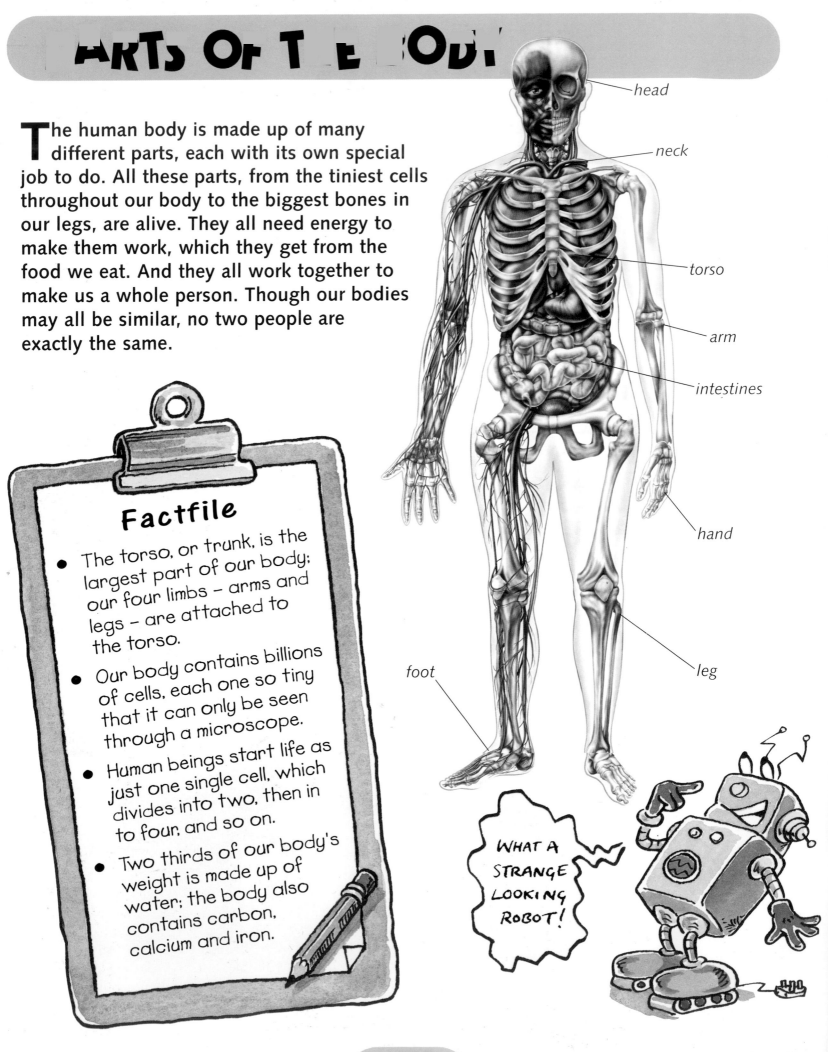

head

neck

torso

arm

intestines

hand

leg

foot

Factfile

- The torso, or trunk, is the largest part of our body; our four limbs – arms and legs – are attached to the torso.

- Our body contains billions of cells, each one so tiny that it can only be seen through a microscope.

- Human beings start life as just one single cell, which divides into two, then in to four, and so on.

- Two thirds of our body's weight is made up of water; the body also contains carbon, calcium and iron.

WHAT A STRANGE LOOKING ROBOT!

Quiz

1 Where in the body is our brain?

2 What is the name of the joint between the arm and hand?

3 How many digits do we have?

4 Human beings are mammals – true or false?

5 What is the central part of a human cell called?

6 Are we warm-blooded or cold-blooded?

Answers

1 In the head. 2 Wrist 3 20 (fingers and toes are digits). 4 True. 5 Nucleus. 6 Warm-blooded.

Body shapes

1. To draw body shapes, you need a big sheet of paper and a friend. Lie face-up on the paper and ask your friend to draw around you with a pencil.

2. Colour in the body with paint and cut out the shape. Glue on eyes, nose, mouth and strips of paper for hair.

3. Draw your friend's shape in the same way. Then you can put your bodies up on the wall. Do they look the same?

SKELETON

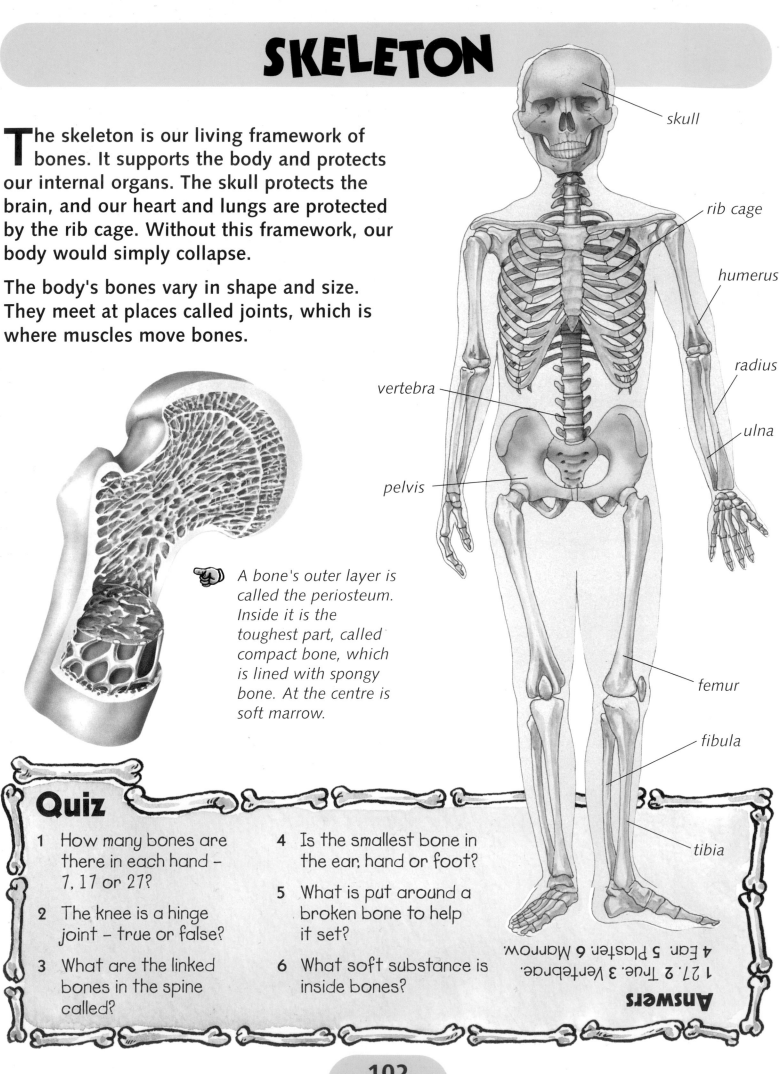

The skeleton is our living framework of bones. It supports the body and protects our internal organs. The skull protects the brain, and our heart and lungs are protected by the rib cage. Without this framework, our body would simply collapse.

The body's bones vary in shape and size. They meet at places called joints, which is where muscles move bones.

skull

rib cage

humerus

radius

ulna

vertebra

pelvis

femur

fibula

tibia

A bone's outer layer is called the periosteum. Inside it is the toughest part, called compact bone, which is lined with spongy bone. At the centre is soft marrow.

Quiz

1 How many bones are there in each hand – 7, 17 or 27?

2 The knee is a hinge joint – true or false?

3 What are the linked bones in the spine called?

4 Is the smallest bone in the ear, hand or foot?

5 What is put around a broken bone to help it set?

6 What soft substance is inside bones?

Answers
1 27. 2 True. 3 Vertebrae. 4 Ear. 5 Plaster. 6 Marrow.

102

Factfile

- An adult has about 206 bones.

- Babies are born with as many as 270 bones; as a child grows, some bones join together.

- The hips and shoulders are called ball-and-socket joints, because that's what they look like and how they work.

- You may be up to a centimetre shorter in the evening than when you wake up in the morning; your spine squashes up slightly as you stand during the day.

- The femur, or thigh bone, is the body's largest bone, making up over a quarter of a person's height.

YOU CAN SEE WHICH IS THE LARGEST BONE IN MY BODY!

Wired-up bones

1. You will need 12 wire coat-hangers to build this skeleton mobile.

2. Pull the bottom of a hanger until it forms an oval face shape. Cover with white crêpe paper and tape it round the neck.

3. Hang the hanger on a high hook and build your mobile in position. Hook each hanger to another and tape it in place. Hook arm hangers to the shoulders and tape on old gloves. Hook foot hangers to the legs and pull on stuffed socks.

4. Draw a face on the crêpe. If you want to make it really creepy, spray your skeleton with white or luminous paint.

MUSCLES

To run or jump, we use our muscles. In fact, muscles make all our body's movements possible, even tiny ones such as blinking or smiling. To do this, muscles shorten and pull on the bones to which they are attached.

Some of our muscles work automatically, without us thinking about it. These include the chest muscles that help us breathe and the muscles in the stomach and intestines that help us digest food.

WOW, D'YOU THINK I'VE GOT ALL THOSE MUSCLES?

Factfile

- The human body has about 620 muscles that it uses for movement.

- You use about 200 muscles every time you take a single step.

- The tiny muscles that help our eyes focus move about 100,000 times a day; you would have to walk about 80 km to give your leg muscles that much exercise.

- More than 30 small muscles in our face allow us to smile, frown and make other expressions.

Muscles work in pairs, such as the biceps and triceps in your upper arm.

biceps

triceps

1 To lift something, the biceps muscle gets shorter.

2 The hinge joint of the elbow moves.

3 To move the arm back down, the triceps shortens and the biceps gets longer.

THE BIGGEST MUSCLES ARE THE BUTTOCKS!

Tug of war

1. To play this muscly game, make up two equal teams – it could be just one on each side.

2. Grab the ends of a strong rope, take up the strain till the rope is taught, and then try to pull each other an agreed distance (say, 2 m).

3. If you are losing, don't let go of the rope. If you did, your opponent would go flying backwards and this could be very dangerous.

BODY ORGANS

The body's organs are parts that do one special job or a series of related jobs. The heart, lungs and brain are all large, important organs. Different bodily organs are all dependent on each other and they work together as a system. The heart and lungs, for example, work together to collect oxygen and deliver it to all parts of the body.

brain

lungs

heart

liver

kidney

stomach

large intestine

small intestine

Factfile

- The word 'organ' comes from the Greek word for 'tool' (something that does a special job).

- There are about a million clumps of tiny blood vessels (or capillaries) inside each kidney.

- An adult's kidneys filter about 1,000 litres of blood every day.

- In 1967 Dr Christiaan Barnard completed the first successful heart transplant operation.

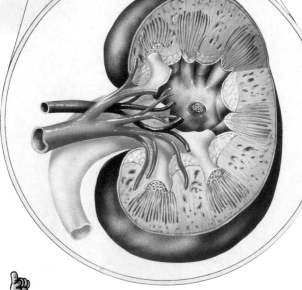

Kidneys clean the blood by removing waste products. Blood is pumped to each of the two kidneys. Inside there are tiny blood vessels, where waste substances are passed into tubes. This waste becomes urine, which moves along the tubes to be stored in the bladder.

Quiz

1 What are our organs of sight called?

2 How many times is our blood cleaned every day by the kidneys – 3, 30 or 300 times?

3 What is a person who gives an organ to someone else called?

4 Scientists are experimenting with using pigs' hearts for human transplants – true or false?

5 Can an artificial kidney machine do the job of damaged kidneys?

6 Which organ makes bile?

Answers
1 Eyes. 2 300 times. 3 Organ donor. 4 True. 5 Yes. 6 Liver.

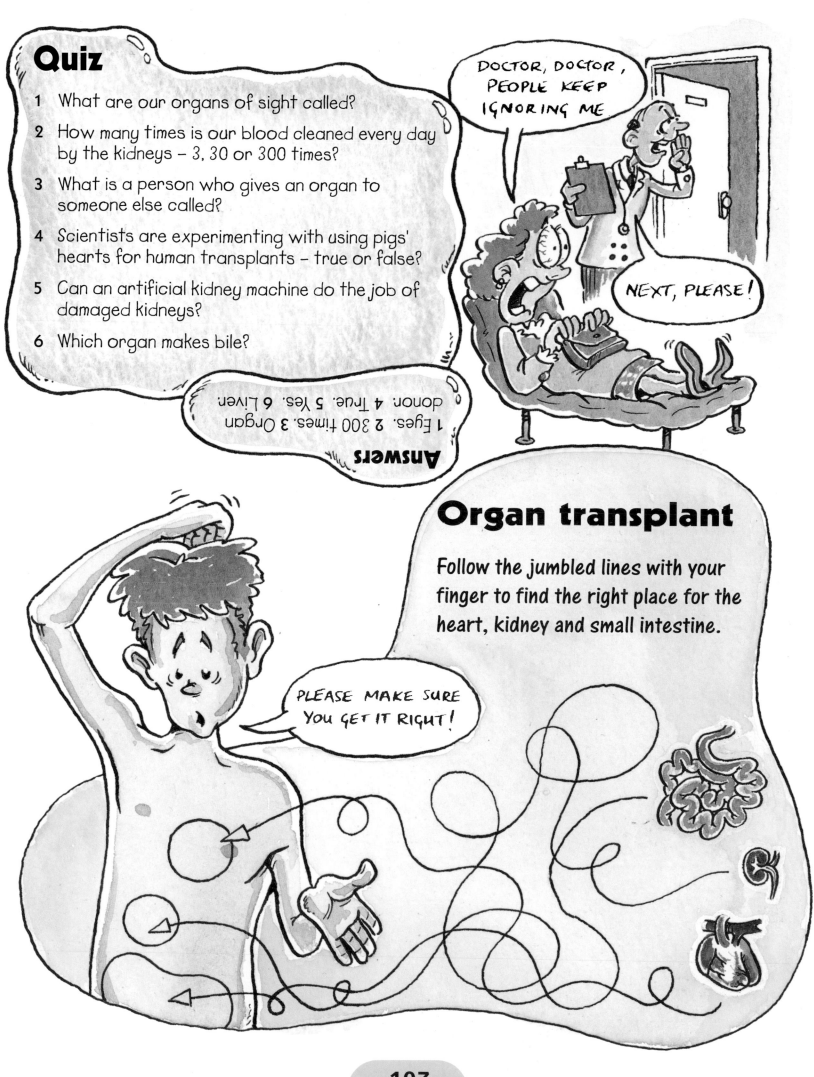

Organ transplant

Follow the jumbled lines with your finger to find the right place for the heart, kidney and small intestine.

BLOOD

The blood in our body carries oxygen from the air we breathe, as well as goodness from the food we eat. It travels in small tubes, called blood vessels, to all parts of the body. Blood is pumped around the body by a powerful muscle called the heart.

aorta

heart

artery

vein

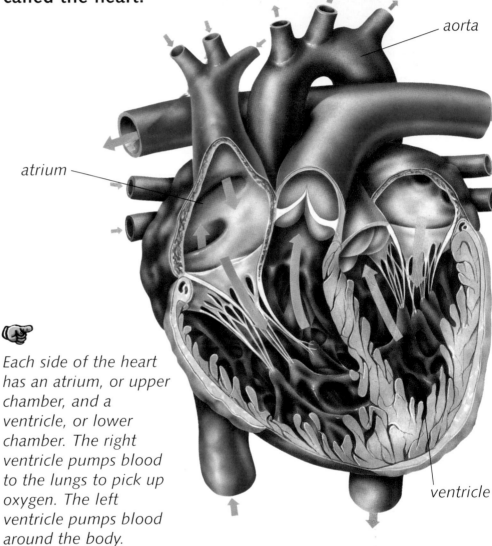

aorta

atrium

ventricle

👉 *Each side of the heart has an atrium, or upper chamber, and a ventricle, or lower chamber. The right ventricle pumps blood to the lungs to pick up oxygen. The left ventricle pumps blood around the body.*

Quiz

1   Which fruit has a similar shape to the heart?
2   The heart lies slightly to which side of your chest?
3   There are three major blood groups – true or false?

4   When you run about, does your heart beat faster or slower?
5   What makes up 90 % of plasma?
6   What are tiny blood vessels called?

1 Pear 2 Left 3 False (there are four). 4 Faster. 5 Water. 6 Capillaries.

Answers

Although our blood looks red, it is mainly made up of a yellowish liquid called plasma. There are three different sorts of cells in the plasma: red cells, which carry oxygen; white cells, which help the body fight disease; and platelets, which help cuts to heal.

red blood cells

white blood cells

platelets

Factfile

- Blood travels away from the heart in blood vessels called arteries (coloured red in our illustration). It travels back to the heart in veins (blue).

- An adult has about five litres of blood.

- An adult's heart pumps more than 7,000 litres of blood around the body every day.

- A substance in red blood cells called haemoglobin makes blood look red.

- A child's heart beats about a hundred times each minute.

Hear the heartbeat

1. To make your own stethoscope, cut the top end off two plastic bottles to make cups.

2. Then push the ends of some hosepipe or other plastic tubing into the two cups.

3. Put one cup over a friend's heart and the other cup over your ear. Can you hear the heartbeat?

BOOM!

BOOM!

BREATHING

When we breathe in, we take air into our body. Air contains a gas called oxygen, and we need this to help make our bodies work. The air we breathe in goes into our lungs, which take the oxygen into very narrow tubes and pass it into our bloodstream. When we breathe out again, the lungs get rid of used air.

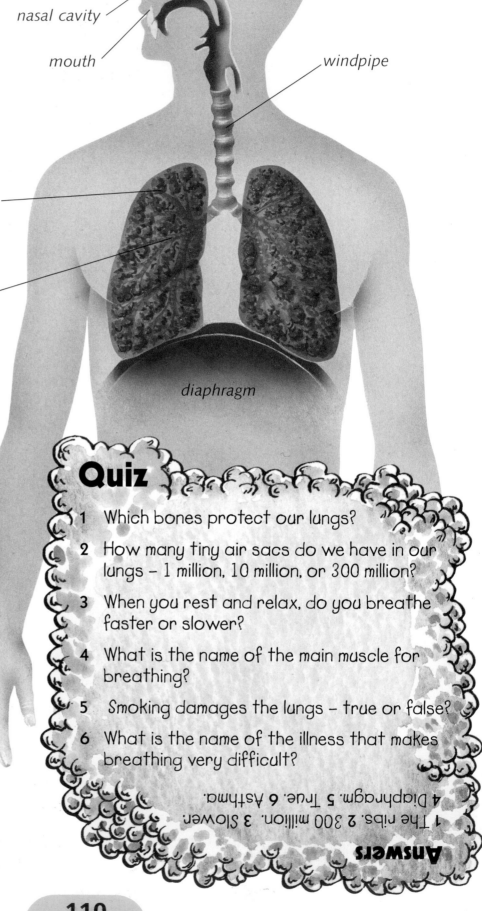

nasal cavity

mouth

windpipe

lung

bronchial tube

diaphragm

IMAGINE BREATHING IN AND OUT THOUSANDS OF TIMES A DAY. IT MAKES ME FEEL TIRED OUT!

Quiz

1 Which bones protect our lungs?

2 How many tiny air sacs do we have in our lungs – 1 million, 10 million, or 300 million?

3 When you rest and relax, do you breathe faster or slower?

4 What is the name of the main muscle for breathing?

5 Smoking damages the lungs – true or false?

6 What is the name of the illness that makes breathing very difficult?

Answers

1 The ribs. 2 300 million. 3 Slower. 4 Diaphragm 5 True. 6 Asthma.

Breathing in and out

As you breathe in, your rib cage expands and a large dome of muscle, called the diaphragm, contracts and flattens.
The lungs then fill up with air.

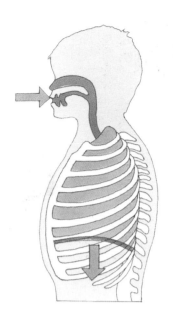

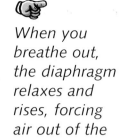 *When you breathe out, the diaphragm relaxes and rises, forcing air out of the lungs.*

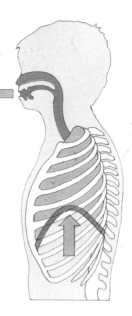

Factfile

- An adult's lungs hold about five litres of air.

- About 21 percent of air is oxygen, which is what our body's cells need most.

- Adults usually breathe about 18 times a minute, or more than 25,000 times a day (or more than nine million times a year!).

- An adult's lungs contain about 300 billion tiny blood vessels, or capillaries; if you laid them end to end, they would stretch over 2,000 km.

Blow football

1. Build matchboxes or building bricks into goalposts, at either end of a table. Put more boxes or bricks along the edge of the table to stop the ball rolling off.

2. Divide the players into teams (one-a-side will do), and give each player a drinking straw. Put a ping-pong ball in the middle of the table. At the first whistle the players try to blow the ball into their opponent's goal.

3. How many goals can you score before running out of puff?

MAKING SOUNDS

All sounds are made by things vibrating, and our voices make sounds by vibrating the vocal cords. These cords are soft flaps in the larynx, or voice box, which is at the back of the throat. When air passes over the vocal cords, they vibrate and make a sound. We then use our tongue and lips to change the sounds and form words.

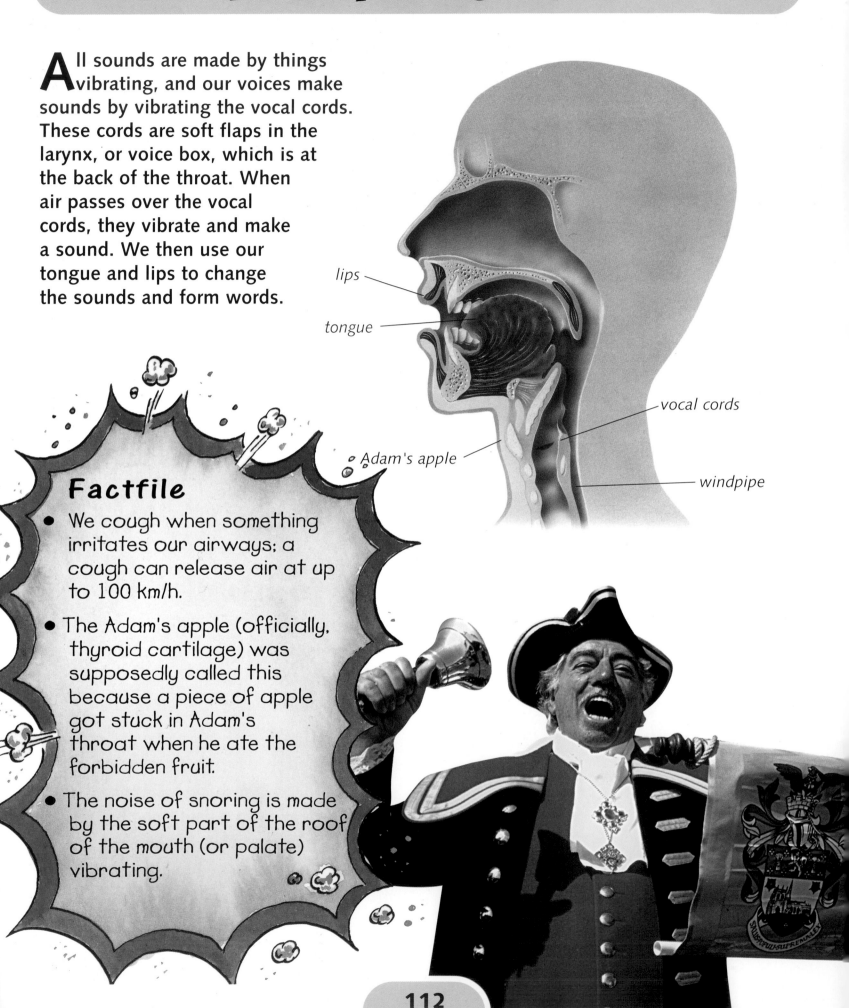

lips

tongue

vocal cords

Adam's apple

windpipe

Factfile

- We cough when something irritates our airways; a cough can release air at up to 100 km/h.

- The Adam's apple (officially, thyroid cartilage) was supposedly called this because a piece of apple got stuck in Adam's throat when he ate the forbidden fruit.

- The noise of snoring is made by the soft part of the roof of the mouth (or palate) vibrating.

Make a loudhailer

1. Bend a thin piece of cardboard (about 40 x 30 cm) into a cone shape and fix it with sticky tape.

2. Cut out a smaller piece of cardboard to cover the gap in the cone. Put it in place and then tape it.

3. Cut both ends of the cone into a neat circle. Now you can use your loudhailer as an amplifier (but warn the neighbours first!).

Vocal cords

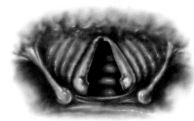

When the cords are apart, air can move freely past them and no sound is made.

Tiny muscles pull the cords together, leaving a small gap. As air is forced through the gap, the cords vibrate and 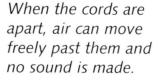 *make sounds.*

Quiz

1. What is your trachea?
2. Do girls have an Eve's apple?
3. How many different languages are spoken in the world today – 40, 400 or 4,000?
4. Which is further back from the mouth, the pharynx or larynx?
5. Which language is spoken by more people than any other?
6. Female larynxes are smaller with tighter cords, and so produce higher voices – true or false?

Answers
1 Your windpipe. 2 No. 3 4,000. 4 Larynx.
5 Chinese. 6 True.

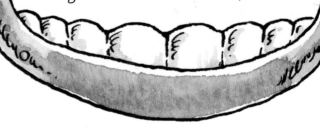

CAN YOU WHISTLE?

PHEPP

BRAIN

The brain, inside our skull, is the body's control centre. It keeps other parts of the body working properly, and is responsible for thoughts, feelings and memory. The brain is linked to the rest of the body by nerves. It receives information in the form of tiny electric currents. The brain 'reads' the information faster and more efficiently than any computer, and then acts on it by sending information back down the nerves.

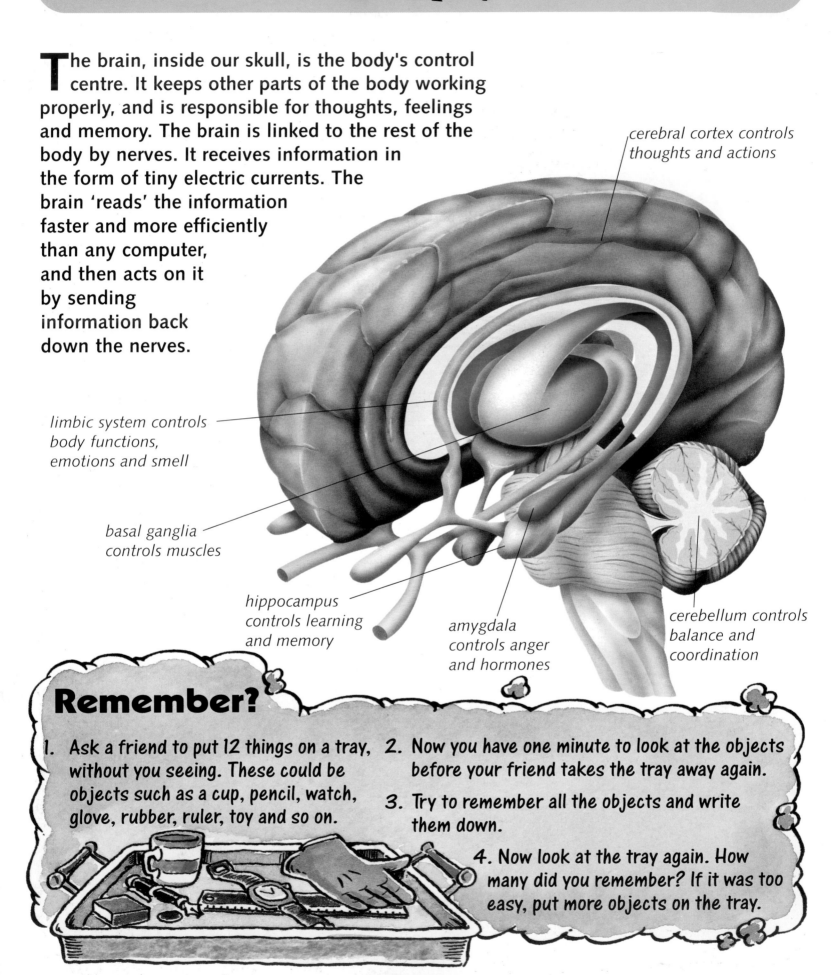

cerebral cortex controls thoughts and actions

limbic system controls body functions, emotions and smell

basal ganglia controls muscles

hippocampus controls learning and memory

amygdala controls anger and hormones

cerebellum controls balance and coordination

Remember?

1. Ask a friend to put 12 things on a tray, without you seeing. These could be objects such as a cup, pencil, watch, glove, rubber, ruler, toy and so on.

2. Now you have one minute to look at the objects before your friend takes the tray away again.

3. Try to remember all the objects and write them down.

4. Now look at the tray again. How many did you remember? If it was too easy, put more objects on the tray.

Factfile

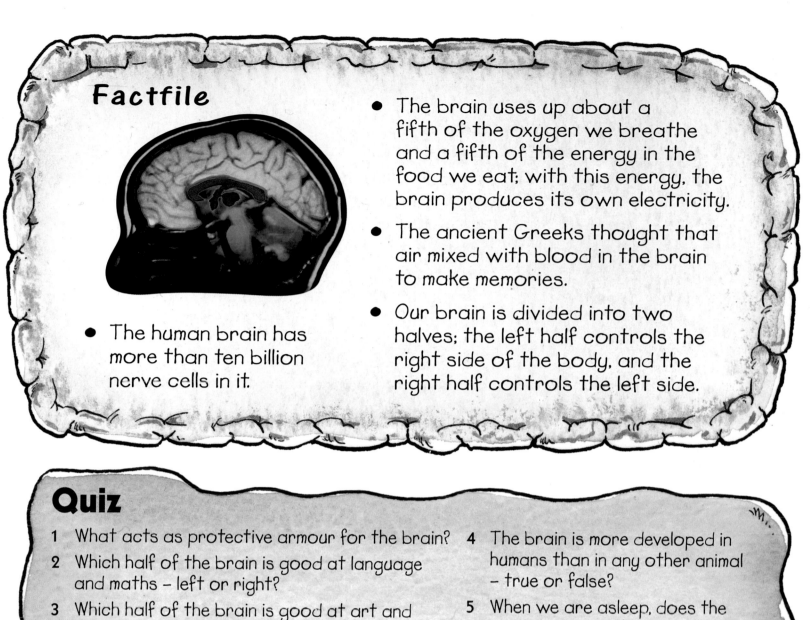

- The human brain has more than ten billion nerve cells in it.

- The brain uses up about a fifth of the oxygen we breathe and a fifth of the energy in the food we eat; with this energy, the brain produces its own electricity.

- The ancient Greeks thought that air mixed with blood in the brain to make memories.

- Our brain is divided into two halves; the left half controls the right side of the body, and the right half controls the left side.

Quiz

1 What acts as protective armour for the brain?
2 Which half of the brain is good at language and maths – left or right?
3 Which half of the brain is good at art and music – left or right?
4 The brain is more developed in humans than in any other animal – true or false?
5 When we are asleep, does the brain go on working?
6 What send messages to the brain along optic nerves?

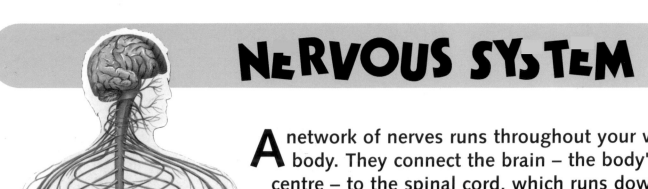

NERVOUS SYSTEM

A network of nerves runs throughout your whole body. They connect the brain – the body's control centre – to the spinal cord, which runs down the body inside the backbone. Together, the brain and spinal cord make up the body's central nervous system. Smaller nerves run from the spinal cord all over the body. The nerves send messages to and from the brain, giving information about the senses.

Reflex action

If you touch a sharp pin, a message goes along a sensory nerve to your spinal cord. A motor nerve then moves your hand away at once. This immediate response is called a reflex action. The message carries on to your brain, which knows about the pain after your hand has moved, so then you feel it.

Factfile

- The medulla lies between the lower part of the brain and the top of the spinal cord; its nerve cells carry messages between the two.

- In adults, the spinal cord is about 40 cm long.

- The spinal cord runs inside the backbone, and the vertebrae that make up the backbone protect it.

- If the spinal cord is broken in an accident, the person is paralyzed because the nerves' messages cannot get through to the brain.

Quiz

1 Is the forebrain at the front or the back?

2 What are neurones?

3 What does CNS stand for?

4 Are humans vertebrates or invertebrates?

5 Can people move as fast as their own nerves' messages?

6 Nerves are in charge of muscles – true or false?

Answers

1 Front. 2 Nerve cells. 3 Central nervous system. 4 Vertebrates (they have a backbone). 5 No. 6 True.

Make a reactometer

1. Divide a long strip of stiff card into seven equal parts. Make each section a different colour.

2. Ask a friend to hold the strip above your hand.

3. Place your thumb and index finger just below the strip and try to pinch the strip as quickly as possible when your friend lets go of it. The closer you catch it to the bottom end, the better your reactions are.

4. Now swap places and test your friend's reactions.

MESSAGES TRAVEL ALONG NERVES AT 400 KILOMETRES AN HOUR.

JUST AS WELL!

SLEEP

Most people spend about a third of their lives asleep. Sleep gives the body time to rest, which is why we sleep more than usual when we are ill. Since muscles have very little work to do when we are asleep, the parts of the brain that control movement can rest too.

We grow when we are asleep, so babies need at least 18 hours of sleep every day. As we get older and grow less, we sleep less.

Quiz

1   Does your heart beat faster or more slowly when you are asleep?

2   What are scary dreams called?

3   What is the name of the fairy-tale character who slept for twenty years?

4   What type of clock wakes people up?

5   Do old people usually need a lot or little sleep?

6   What does REM stand for?

Answers
1 More slowly. 2 Nightmares.
3 Rip Van Winkle. 4 Alarm clock.
5 Little. 6 Rapid eye movement.

👉 *In the traditional tale, Rip Van Winkle falls into a deep sleep for 20 years. When he finally wakes up, he can't understand why the world is so different.*

Factfile

- Some adults only need a couple of hours sleep every night.

- People who sleepwalk get out of bed and walk about while they are asleep; they usually don't remember anything about it next morning.

- We don't always remember our dreams the next morning, but everyone dreams for up to a quarter of the time they are asleep.

- When we dream, our eyes move about rapidly behind our closed eyelids.

- Yawning is infectious: if you see someone yawn, you usually want to do it too.

Sleep chart

1. Take a large sheet of paper and mark it off into four rows of seven squares. Each square is a day, and each row is a week.

2. Just before you go to bed each evening, write the time in a square. Then next morning write in what time you got up.

3. When you've filled the chart, you can check out how many hours you've slept in a whole month.

sleep chart

mon	tue	wed	thur	fri	sat	sun
7.45	7.30	7.32	7.56	8.00	7.52	8.20
9.00	8.45	8.35	8.52	8.30	9.10	9.30
7.34	7.32	7.21	8.00	7.15	7.18	8.30
8.35	8.56	8.45	8.15	8.32	9.00	8.56
7.32	7.21	8.00	7.15	7.32	7.18	8.30
8.56	8.45	8.15	8.32	9.00	8.56	8.23
7.15	7.32	7.18	8.30	7.32	7.21	8.00
9.00	8.56	8.23	8.56	8.45	8.15	8.32

SKIN

The skin is our body's protection from the outside world. It keeps out dirt, water and germs, as well as shielding us from the Sun's burning rays. Much of our body is made of water, and the skin stops the body from drying out.

Our skin is full of nerve endings, which send messages to the brain with information about such important things as pain, heat and cold.

The inner layer, called the dermis, contains masses of nerve endings.

hair erector muscle

hair follicle

The tough outer layer of the skin, called the epidermis, is waterproof and germ-proof.

keratin layer

epidermis

hair

sweat gland

Quiz

1 What are little brown sun-spots on the skin called?

2 Do our fingers give ten different fingerprints?

3 What is a skin specialist called?

4 Do you sweat more when you're hot or cold?

5 Skin colour comes from a substance called lanolin – true or false?

6 Do you shiver when you're hot or cold?

Every single person in the whole world has slightly different fingerprints.

arch

loop

whorl

DON'T FORGET TO CHECK OUT THE ARCHES AND LOOPS.

Hand and foot prints

1. Use ready-mixed paint thickened with a little PVA glue and paint your palms and fingers with it. Then press your hands down firmly on a sheet of paper.

2. Wash your hands then roll out a long strip of paper on the floor. Take off your shoes and socks and step into a tray of the paint. Then walk to the other end of the paper.

3. Compare your prints with a friend's. Can you see the difference? Use a magnifying glass for a really close look.

Factfile

- The thickest skin (about 3 mm) is on the palms of your hands and soles of your feet.

- We sweat to keep cool; produced by glands in the dermis, sweat takes heat from the body and helps cool it down as it dries on the skin.

- We get goose bumps when tiny hairs stand up and pull the skin up around them; the hairs help keep you warm by trapping air next to your skin.

I'M VERY THICK SKINNED

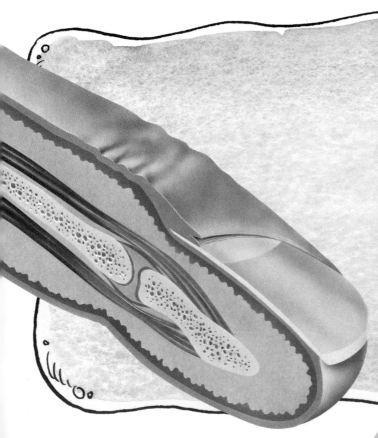

We have hair all over our bodies, except on the palms of our hands and the soles of our feet. Most of the hairs are too fine and tiny to see properly. Hairs give our skin extra warmth and protection. The hair on our head grows thickest and longest.

Our nails are there to protect the tips of our fingers and toes. Both nails and hair are made from a tough substance called keratin.

 Hairs grow from follicles in the dermis of the skin.

Wavy hair grows from oval follicles.

Curly hair grows from rectangular follicles.

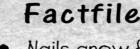

Straight hair grows from round follicles.

Factfile

- Nails grow from the base, under the skin; the pale half-moon is new nail that has just grown.

- An Indian man grew all his fingernails to over a metre long.

- The hair on your head grows about 3 mm each week, or 15 cm a year.

- Most fair-haired people have about 140,000 hairs on their head; people with brown hair have about 120,000; and redheads have just 90,000.

- About 50 hairs fall out of a person's head every day.

122

Quiz

1 Hair colour comes from a substance called gelatine – true or false?

2 How long do nails usually grow in a month – 1, 3 or 7 mm?

3 Do babies have fingernails before they are born?

4 Was the world's longest beard over 1, 3 or 5 m long?

5 Does a haircut hurt?

6 What is the thin strip of skin at the base of a nail called?

Answers

1 False (it's melanin, the same as skin). 2 3 mm. 3 Yes. 4 Over 5 m. 5 No (if it does, change your hairdresser). 6 Cuticle.

EEK!

I'D BE HAPPY WITH ANY KIND OF HAIR!

Green hair

1. Cut the top off a pumpkin and scoop out some of the flesh. Fill the pumpkin with a layer of cotton wool.

2. Moisten the cotton wool with water and sow cress seeds on it. Now draw a happy face on your pumpkin with black marker pen.

3. Keep the seeds and seedlings watered and watch your pumpkin's green hair grow.

TEETH

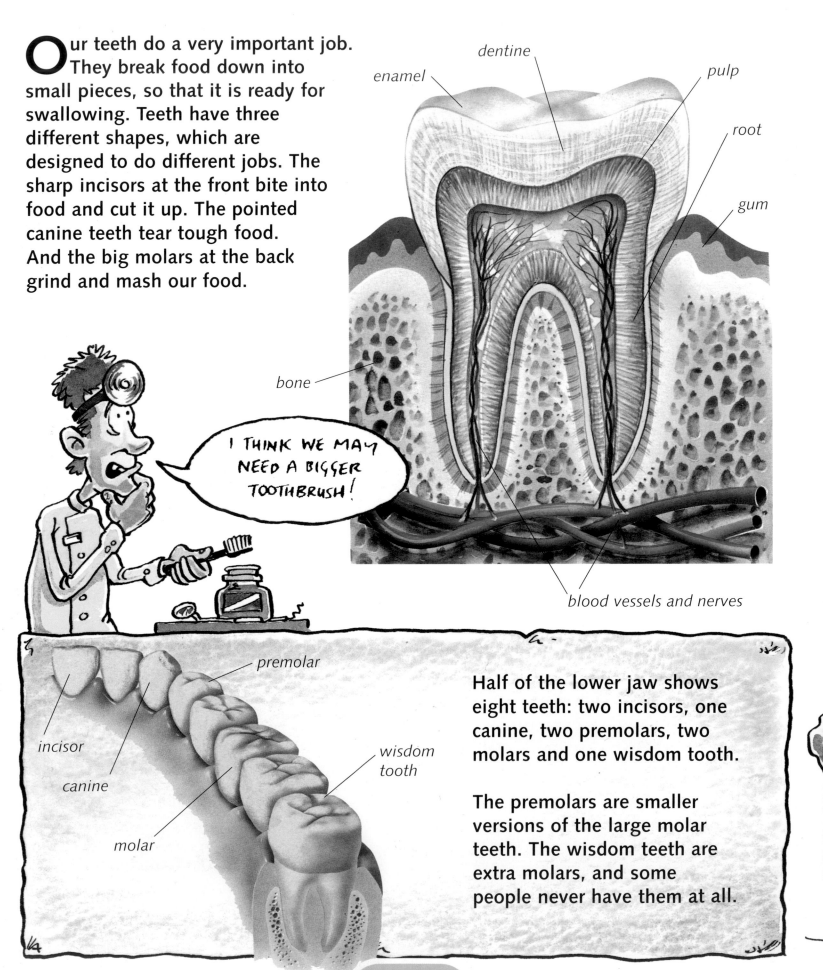

Our teeth do a very important job. They break food down into small pieces, so that it is ready for swallowing. Teeth have three different shapes, which are designed to do different jobs. The sharp incisors at the front bite into food and cut it up. The pointed canine teeth tear tough food. And the big molars at the back grind and mash our food.

dentine

enamel

pulp

root

gum

bone

blood vessels and nerves

I THINK WE MAY NEED A BIGGER TOOTHBRUSH!

premolar

incisor

canine

molar

wisdom tooth

Half of the lower jaw shows eight teeth: two incisors, one canine, two premolars, two molars and one wisdom tooth.

The premolars are smaller versions of the large molar teeth. The wisdom teeth are extra molars, and some people never have them at all.

Quiz

1 What can you wear on your teeth to make them straight?

2 What are a young child's first teeth called?

3 What is caries?

4 Are people with wisdom teeth really wiser?

5 What is a tooth doctor called?

6 New-born babies don't usually have teeth – true or false?

Answers

1 A brace. 2 Milk teeth. 3 Tooth decay. 4 No (though they disagree!) 5 Dentist. 6 True.

Egg decay

1. This an experiment to see how acid can attack your teeth if it is left untouched.

2. Put an eggshell into a small glass or jar of vinegar (which is an acid). Leave it for a couple of days to see what happens.

3. Now you can see why it's good to brush your teeth!

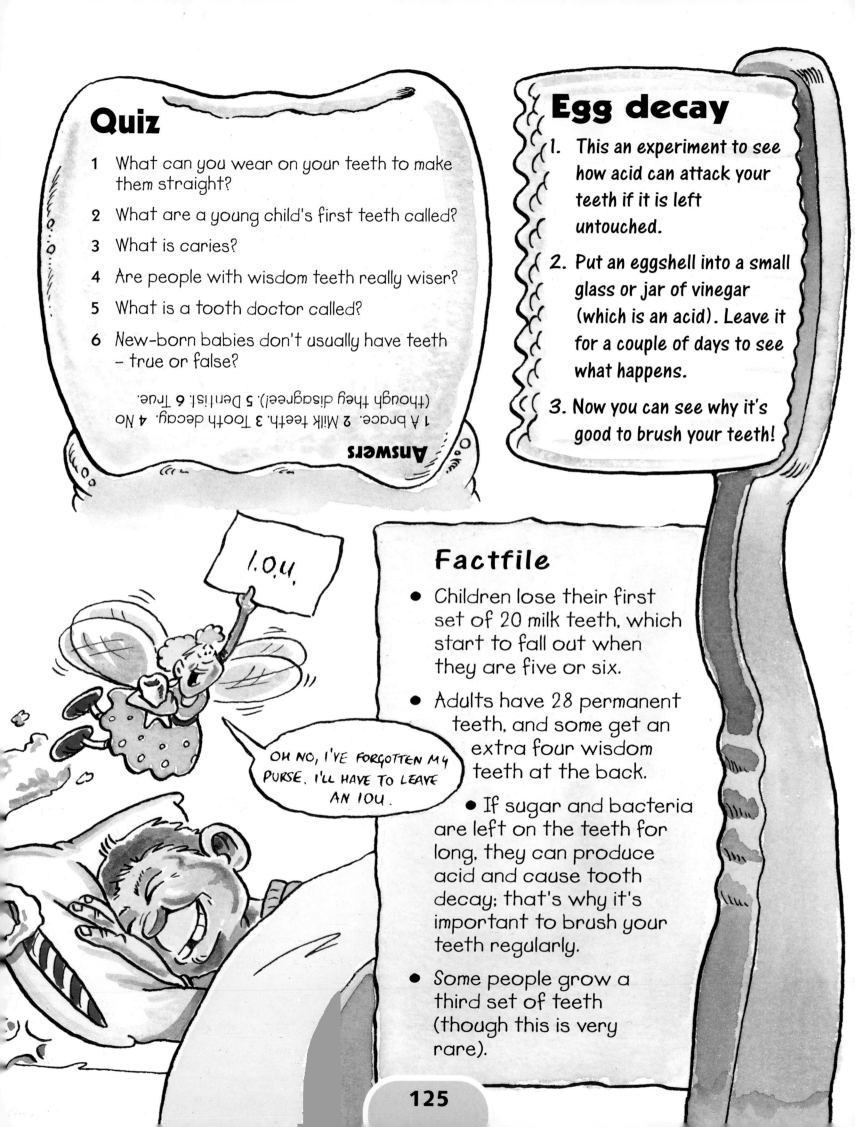

I.O.U.

OH NO, I'VE FORGOTTEN MY PURSE. I'LL HAVE TO LEAVE AN IOU.

Factfile

- Children lose their first set of 20 milk teeth, which start to fall out when they are five or six.

- Adults have 28 permanent teeth, and some get an extra four wisdom teeth at the back.

- If sugar and bacteria are left on the teeth for long, they can produce acid and cause tooth decay; that's why it's important to brush your teeth regularly.

- Some people grow a third set of teeth (though this is very rare).

DIGESTION

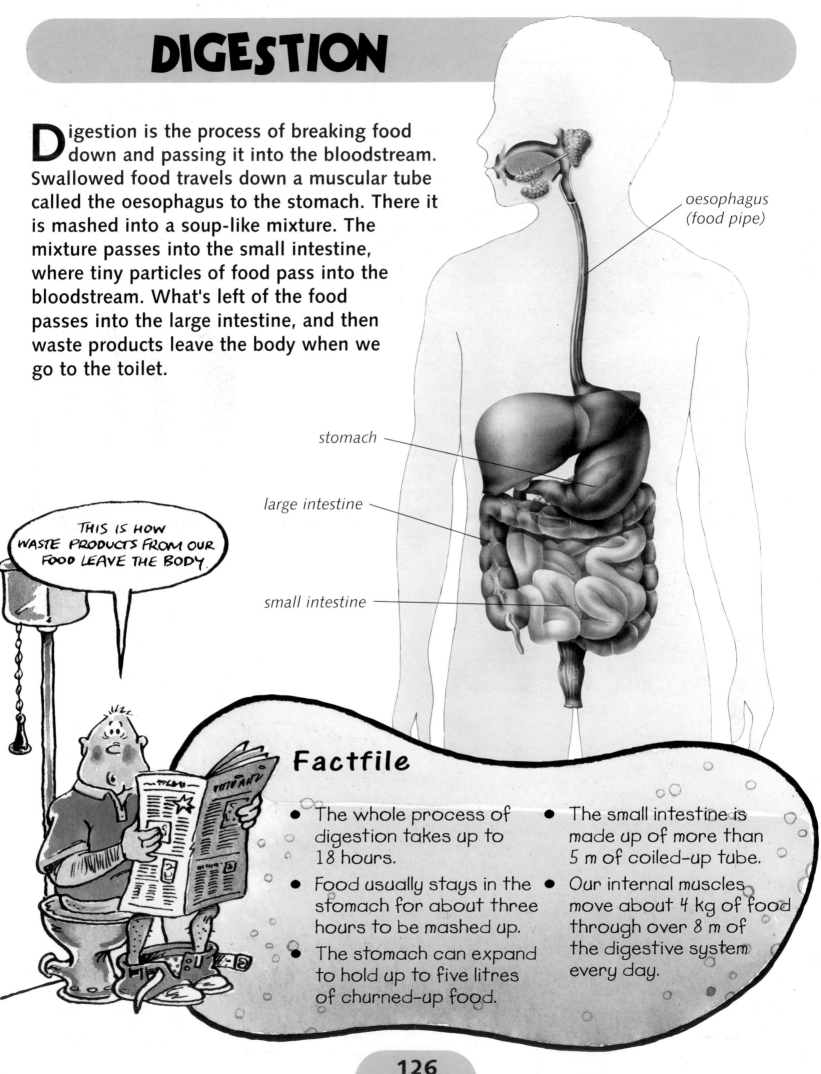

Digestion is the process of breaking food down and passing it into the bloodstream. Swallowed food travels down a muscular tube called the oesophagus to the stomach. There it is mashed into a soup-like mixture. The mixture passes into the small intestine, where tiny particles of food pass into the bloodstream. What's left of the food passes into the large intestine, and then waste products leave the body when we go to the toilet.

oesophagus (food pipe)

stomach

large intestine

small intestine

THIS IS HOW WASTE PRODUCTS FROM OUR FOOD LEAVE THE BODY.

Factfile

- The whole process of digestion takes up to 18 hours.

- Food usually stays in the stomach for about three hours to be mashed up.

- The stomach can expand to hold up to five litres of churned-up food.

- The small intestine is made up of more than 5 m of coiled-up tube.

- Our internal muscles move about 4 kg of food through over 8 m of the digestive system every day.

Find the food

Enter the maze with your finger, and see if you can find your way to a tasty meal.

Quiz

1 What carries the energy from food to all parts of the body?

2 Which is longer, the large or small intestine?

3 What is liquid waste called?

4 Which is wider, the large or small intestine?

5 Does chewing food well help digestion?

6 The stomach is an expandable organ – true or false?

DON'T FORGET TO CHEW AT LEAST 40 TIMES!

Answers

1 Blood. 2 Small intestine. 3 Urine. 4 Large intestine. 5 Yes. 6 True.

FOOD AND DRINK

Our bodies need important substances, called nutrients, which we get from food and drink. These nutrients help us to grow and help the body repair damaged cells, as well as providing energy. We need energy to live and be active.

It is important that we have a balanced diet, so that we don't miss out on any essential nutrients. This means we must eat food from various groups – carbohydrates, proteins, fats and fibre, as well as vitamins and minerals. They are all useful in different ways.

carbohydrates

proteins

fats

fibre

vitamins and minerals

Factfile

- Carbohydrates give us the sort of instant energy that we can use very quickly.

- Proteins are used to make body cells and they help us stay strong.

- Fats give us energy that can be stored by the body to be used later.

- Fibre helps other foods pass more easily through the digestive system.

- The body also needs lots of water – to make blood and sweat, and to carry wastes from the body in urine.

Quiz

1 Which vitamin do oranges give us lots of?

2 Which English cheese comes from the same place as a famous gorge?

3 Which drink has lots of calcium?

4 Which food group does pasta belong to?

5 What is milk without fat called?

6 What are wheat, barley and maize?

Answers

1 Vitamin C. 2 Cheddar. 3 Milk. 4 Carbohydrates. 5 Skimmed milk. 6 Cereals.

WE'RE EATING A BALANCED MEAL!

Salad face

1. Healthy foods can be fun.

2. Salad girl's face is made of mashed potatoes spread out on a plate, hard-boiled eggs, tomatoes, parsley, cress, cucumber, carrots and radishes.

3. With her long chive eyelashes, olive eyes and curly lettuce hair, she's almost too good to eat.

SMELL AND TASTE

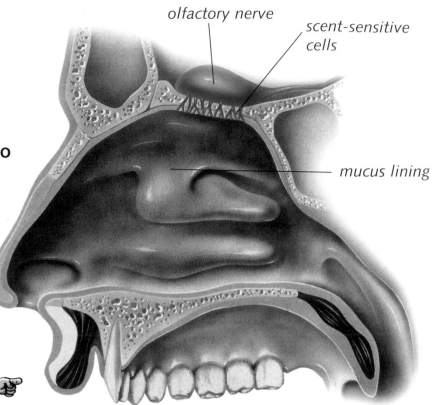

olfactory nerve

scent-sensitive cells

mucus lining

Smell and taste are both very important senses. Our sense of smell is much stronger than that of taste. When we smell something, tiny scent particles go into our nose, which sends messages along a special nerve to the brain. When we taste food, we rely on its smell and texture to give us information about it. The tongue also sends messages to the brain. So when we eat something, the tongue and nose combine to help us enjoy it.

Scent particles dissolve in the mucus lining, and the cells at the top of the nose send signals along the olfactory (or smelling) nerve. This leads to a special part of the brain.

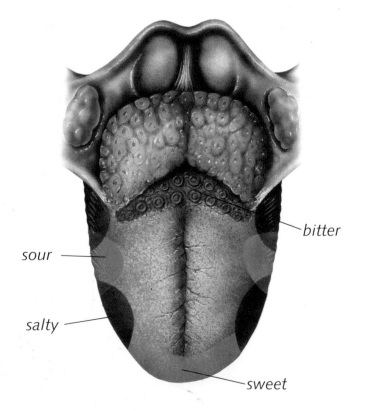

bitter

sour

salty

sweet

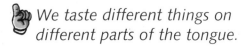
We taste different things on different parts of the tongue.

GAGA SMELL!

Factfile

- When we sneeze, we clear the nose of unwanted particles, such as dust; the explosive rush of air made by a sneeze can reach 160 km/h!

- There are about 10,000 taste buds on our tongue; they are tiny sense organs that help us taste things.

- Babies have taste buds all over the inside of their mouth, and they are very sensitive to smells.

- When you have a cold, you can't taste food properly; this is because your nose is blocked and you can't smell much.

Quiz

1 Which sense is stronger, smell or taste?

2 Does honey taste bitter or sweet?

3 Dogs have a better sense of smell than people – true or false?

4 Does a big nose smell more than a small nose?

5 What does the olfactory area of the brain specialize in?

6 Which taste do we get from the tip of the tongue?

Answers
1 Smell. 2 Sweet 3 True. 4 No. 5 Smells. 6 Sweet.

CALL YOURSELF A SNIFFER DOG!

SNIFF! SNIFF!

Testing taste

1. See how well you can taste things without the help of your nose.

2. Cut an apple, a carrot and some hard cheese into small pieces.

3. Cover your eyes with a blindfold and hold your nose while a friend gives you the pieces of food one by one. Can you tell which is which by taste? Now try the same with other foods.

131

HEARING

Sound waves travel through the air. The outer part of our ear – the part we can see – is shaped to collect the sound waves and pass them into the auditory canal. All sounds are made by things vibrating, and inside the ear the sound waves make a thin sheet of skin, called the eardrum, vibrate. The vibrations are passed on further until nerve endings pick them up and send messages to the brain, so that we 'hear' the sounds.

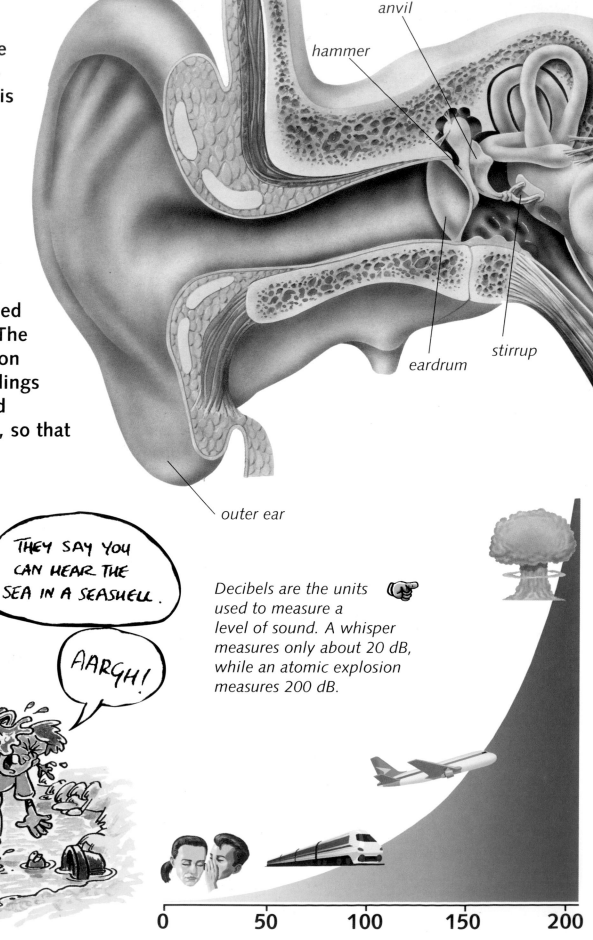

anvil

hammer

eardrum

stirrup

outer ear

THEY SAY YOU CAN HEAR THE SEA IN A SEASHELL.

AARGH!

Decibels are the units used to measure a level of sound. A whisper measures only about 20 dB, while an atomic explosion measures 200 dB.

| 0 | 50 | 100 | 150 | 200 |

Ear-drum

1. Cut a large sheet from a plastic bag. Stretch the sheet over a big tin and put a rubber band around it.

2. Sprinkle sugar onto the plastic.

3. Hold a metal tray next to the drum and beat it with a wooden spoon.

4. The grains of sugar will hop and jump as your drum vibrates with the sound. Just like a real eardrum!

cochlea

Factfile

- The cochlea contains a fluid which moves tiny hairs that send signals to the brain.

- Sometimes our ears 'pop' in a plane or lift; this happens when air pressure outside changes and is equalized in the middle ear.

- The tubular canals next to the cochlea let the brain know what movements the body is making and so help us with balance.

- Sound travels at about 1,225 km/h.

Quiz

1 Do sound messages travel along the auditory or the oral nerve?

2 Which is the smallest bone in the ear (and the whole body)?

3 Dogs hear a greater range of sounds than humans – true or false?

4 Is your balance better or worse when your ears are blocked?

5 Which world-famous German composer was deaf?

6 Which of the ear bones is the incus?

Answers
1 Auditory.
2 Stirrup bone.
3 True. 4 Worse.
5 Beethoven.
6 Anvil bone.

SEEING

We see through our eyes. When light comes into each eye, it passes through a lens, which bends it very precisely. The light rays form an image on an area at the back of the eye called the retina. This image is upside down. Light-sensitive cells in the retina send messages along nerves to the brain. The brain then turns the image around so that we see things the right way up.

When there is very bright light, our pupils are small. But when there is less light, the pupils open more and grow bigger, to let more light in. ☛

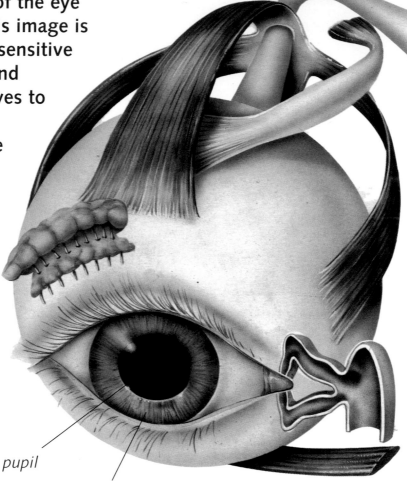

retina

optic nerve

pupil

iris

Quiz

1 Are there more colour-blind men or women?

2 What is the clear protective layer that covers the pupil called?

3 What are contact lenses made of?

4 Some people never blink – true or false?

5 Which sees better, an elephant or an eagle?

6 Who do you see to have your eyes tested?

Answers
1 Men. 2 Cornea. 3 Plastic.
4 False. 5 Eagle. 6 An optician.

Experience the blind spot

1. Cover your left eye and look at the dog.

2. Now move the book slowly towards you. What happens to the cat? It should disappear and then reappear, as it passes the blind spot.

3. Try the same experiment, but this time move the book away from you.

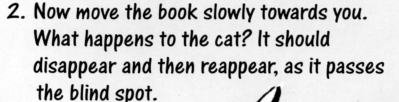

cornea

lens

iris

THAT BULL MUST BE COLOUR-BLIND!

Factfile

- Some people find it difficult to tell the difference between colours, especially red and green; we call this colour blindness.

- Our eyes are about the size of ping-pong balls.

- The coloured part of our eye is called the iris; we inherit the colour of our eyes from our parents.

- You normally blink about 15 times each minute (to keep the eyes moist and clean).

TOUCHING

Our sense of touch gives us a lot of information about the world, allowing us to learn about things around us without seeing them. When we touch things, nerve endings under the surface of the skin send instant messages to the brain. Our brain interprets the messages, and we feel things – such as hardness or softness, or heat or cold, as well as pain or pleasurable sensations.

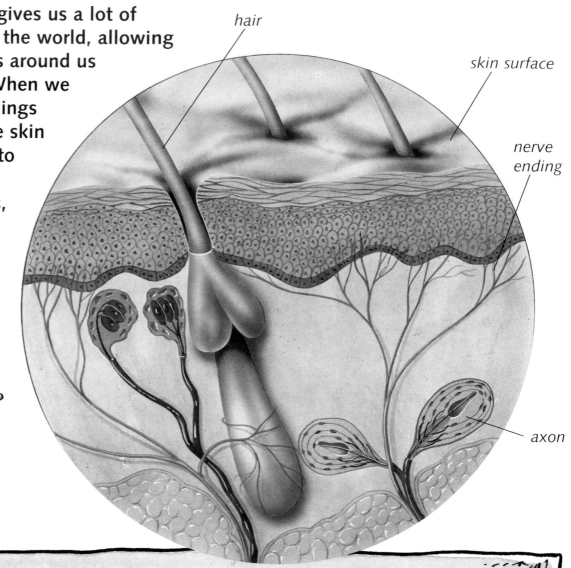

hair

skin surface

nerve ending

axon

Nerve endings lie just beneath the surface of the skin. They send messages to the central nervous system along threadlike axons.

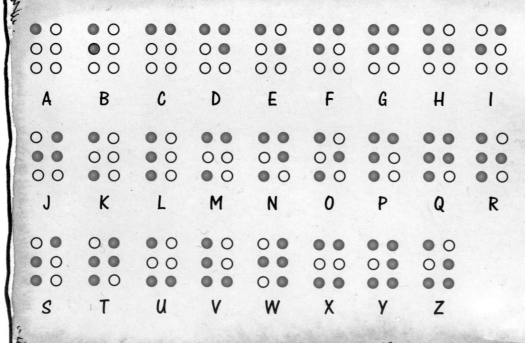

A B C D E F G H I

J K L M N O P Q R

S T U V W X Y Z

Blind people can read by using a system called Braille. The letters of their special alphabet are raised dots that the fingers can touch and feel.

Quiz

1. Does a special part of the brain deal with touch?

2. Many keyboards have raised dots so that typists can feel where their fingers are – true or false?

3. What is a typist who can type without looking at the keys called?

4. Is our sense of touch generally less sensitive in cold weather?

5. What is the name for a computer monitor that operates by touch?

6. Are some people more sensitive to pain than others?

OOH STOP IT, THAT TICKLES!

Factfile

- The Braille system was named after its French inventor, Louis Braille (1809–52), who went blind at the age of three and later became an organ player and a professor.

- We have most nerve endings beneath our fingertips, and the soles of our feet also have many nerves.

- We feel pain to stay safe; it's like an alarm that goes off to tell us that something is wrong.

Play it by feel

1. Collect lots of objects that feel and look different: a sweet, feather, apple, biscuit, ball, stone and so on.

2. Put a blindfold over your friend's eyes and ask him or her to describe the objects just by touching them. Can they guess what each object is?

3. Now ask your friend to put together a different collection so that you can play it by feel.

Each of us began life as a tiny cell inside our mother's body. One of our father's cells joined up with one of our mother's egg-cells. The egg-cell then divided to make more cells and kept on growing to make a baby.

Babies grow in a special part of a mother's body called the womb. As the baby gets bigger, the pregnant mother's womb stretches. After about nine months, the baby is ready to be born.

5 weeks

8 weeks

The fertilized 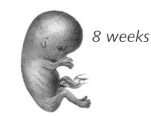 *cell develops into an embryo. After eight weeks, the growing embryo is called a foetus.*

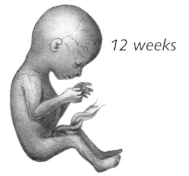

12 weeks

Quiz

1   Are two twins always the same sex?

2   What are five babies born together called?

3   What is the name of the cord that connects a mother to her growing baby?

4   What's the proper word for tummy button?

5   Which organs produce a woman's egg cells?

6   A person specially trained to help women in childbirth is called a midwife – true or false?

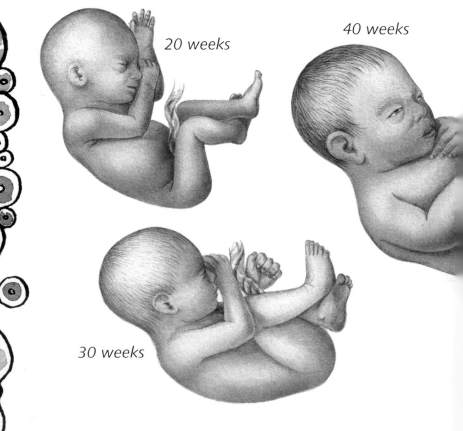

20 weeks

40 weeks

30 weeks

4 Navel. 5 Ovaries. 6 True.
1 No. 2 Quintuplets. 3 Umbilical cord.

Answers

- According to official records from the 1900s, a Russian woman had 69 children, including four sets of quadruplets (four babies); this is a world record.

- After about eight weeks in the womb, a growing baby has all its important body organs, although it is only 4 cm long.

- Inside the womb a baby floats in a watery fluid and gets food and oxygen from its mother through a special cord.

Triplets are three brothers or sisters who develop from three eggs fertilized at the same time.

THREE BABIES BORN TOGETHER ARE CALLED TRIPLETS.

Spot the difference

There are six differences between these two twins.

Can you find them all?

GROWING UP

Tiny babies cannot look after themselves, so they need lots of love and care. But they grow and learn very quickly, first crawling and then taking their first proper steps. By the time a child is two years old, it can do a lot of things for itself. By then the child is already half the height it will be as an adult.

Factfile

- The world's tallest person was American Robert Wadlow; he was taller than most adults by the age of ten, and finally reached a height of 2.72 m.

- The tallest woman was Zeng Jinlian, of China, who measured 2.48 m.

- The oldest person in the world was Frenchwoman Jeanne Calment, who died in 1997 at the age of 122.

- Adults slow up as they get older because their bodies do not use energy as efficiently and their cells cannot replace themselves as quickly.

Quiz

1 How old are people in their teens?

2 In most modern societies, children have to go to school – true or false?

3 What is the word for a child who is just beginning to walk?

4 When old people retire, what do they stop doing?

5 Thousands of years ago in ancient Egypt, children had no toys and games – true or false?

6 At what age is a child usually three quarters of its adult height?

Answers
1 13 to 19. 2 True.
3 Toddler. 4 Working.
5 False (they had lots). 6 Nine.

I'd love to meet someone over two metres tall!

As children go on to become teenagers and young adults, they also grow more independent and start to make all their own decisions. As adults, they may leave their parents and eventually have children of their own.

Height chart

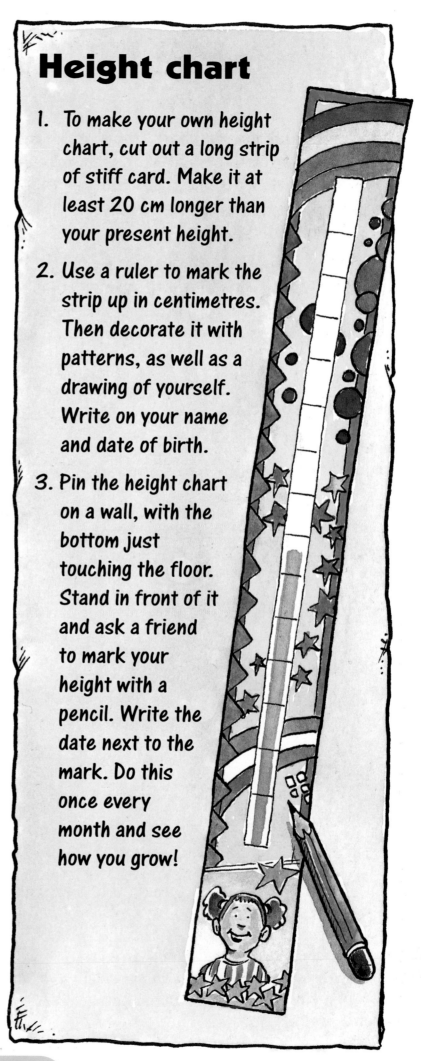

1. To make your own height chart, cut out a long strip of stiff card. Make it at least 20 cm longer than your present height.

2. Use a ruler to mark the strip up in centimetres. Then decorate it with patterns, as well as a drawing of yourself. Write on your name and date of birth.

3. Pin the height chart on a wall, with the bottom just touching the floor. Stand in front of it and ask a friend to mark your height with a pencil. Write the date next to the mark. Do this once every month and see how you grow!

KEEPING HEALTHY

To stay healthy, we have to look after our bodies. We must make sure that we eat properly, take lots of exercise and get as much sleep and rest as we need. We must also wash and stay clean.

Sometimes there is nothing you can do to stop yourself falling ill. But if you normally lead a healthy life, you will probably get better much more quickly than if you didn't.

Stretching your muscles before exercise can help to prevent injury.

Dancing and other similar activities can help to make you more supple and improve your stamina.

Factfile

- Today we can have vaccinations to stop us getting certain diseases; this gives us a mild, harmless form of the disease that builds up our resistance.

- People today live much longer than they ever did in the past, especially in the richer parts of the world.

- Smoking cigarettes, drinking too much alcohol and taking any non-medical drugs all damage the body and can ruin your health.

Quiz

1 What is the name for vigorous exercises that help the body increase its intake of oxygen?

2 Which vehicle takes people to hospital in an emergency?

3 What is an arachnophobic person afraid of?

4 Which country has the most hospitals?

5 What does a doctor write out to give us medicine?

6 Which sport is played with a shuttlecock?

Answers

1 Aerobics. 2 An ambulance.
3 Spiders. 4 China. 5 A prescription.
6 Badminton.

DANCING IS SUCH GOOD EXERCISE!

Warming up

It's very important to warm your muscles up before you do strenuous exercise. Here are some good ways to warm up. Do each of them five times.

1. Stretch your arms above your head, then squat and swing your arms between your legs

2. Pull each knee in turn up towards your chest (this is good for your knees, thighs and hips.

3. With legs slightly apart, lift each arm in turn and bend towards the other side.

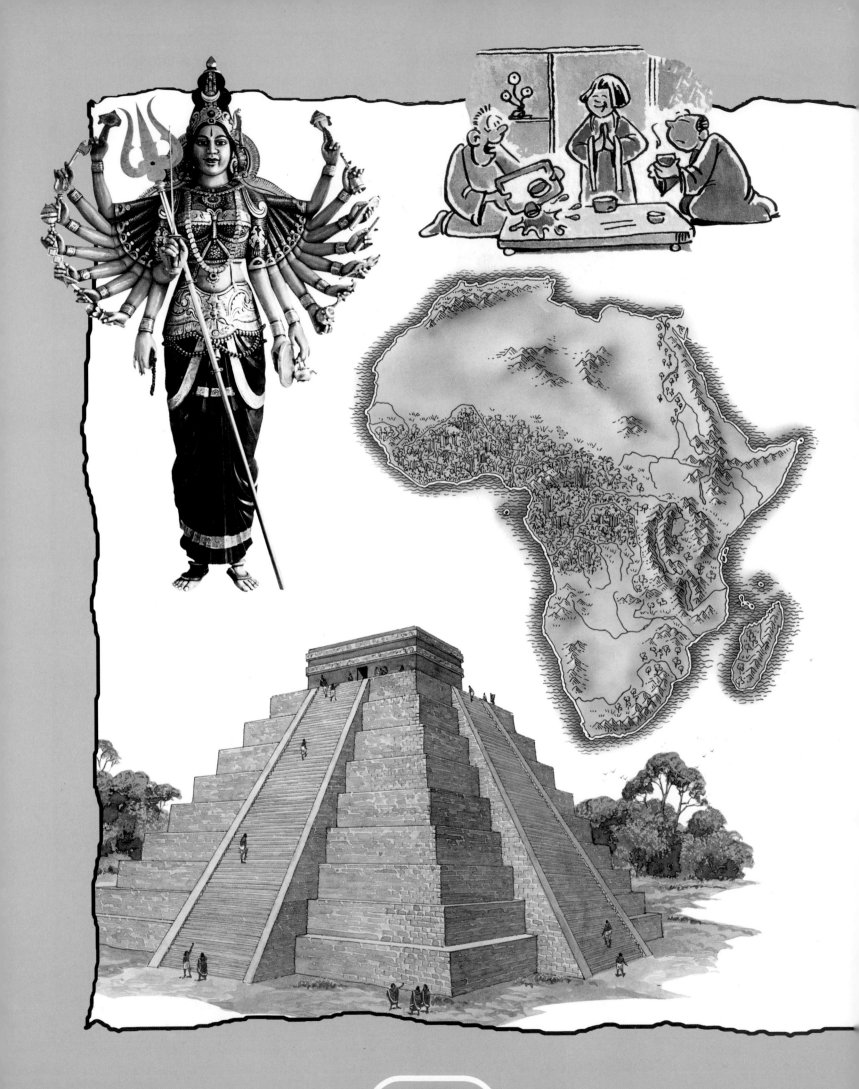

OUR WONDERFUL WORLD

The six billion people of the world live on six different continents, all of which have their own special landscapes and famous places. Some people live in wet rainforests and others in dry deserts. Some live in the warm tropics, others in the freezing polar regions, and while some people live in small villages, many others make up the population of huge, crowded cities. Wherever they live, people have their own language, religion and customs. Have fun finding out how and where people live – all over the world.

T E WORLD'S E VIRONMENTS

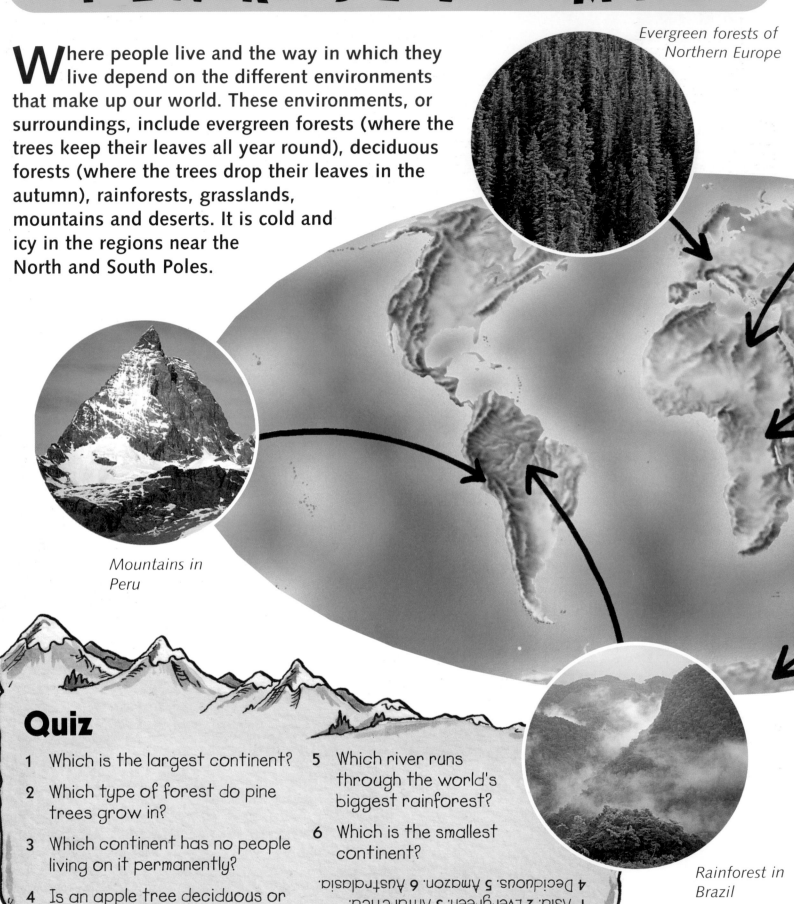

Where people live and the way in which they live depend on the different environments that make up our world. These environments, or surroundings, include evergreen forests (where the trees keep their leaves all year round), deciduous forests (where the trees drop their leaves in the autumn), rainforests, grasslands, mountains and deserts. It is cold and icy in the regions near the North and South Poles.

Evergreen forests of Northern Europe

Mountains in Peru

Rainforest in Brazil

Quiz

1 Which is the largest continent?

2 Which type of forest do pine trees grow in?

3 Which continent has no people living on it permanently?

4 Is an apple tree deciduous or evergreen?

5 Which river runs through the world's biggest rainforest?

6 Which is the smallest continent?

Answers
1 Asia. 2 Evergreen. 3 Antarctica. 4 Deciduous. 5 Amazon. 6 Australasia.

Find their way home

Can you match the people to their homes? One comes from a very cold environment, another from the plains, and the third lives in a big city. Which home is left as the odd one out?

A.

B.

C.

D.

Answers
1.C 2.D 3.A
B is the odd one out!

1.

2.

3.

Deserts of North Africa

Grasslands of central Africa

Polar region of Antarctica

PEOPLE TRADITIONALLY BUILD HOMES OF LOCAL MATERIALS.

Factfile

- The world's land is divided into seven continents: Africa, Antarctica, Asia, Australasia, Europe, North America and South America.

- The area around the North Pole is called the Arctic; it is covered by the Arctic Ocean, which is frozen at the surface.

- The area around the South Pole is the continent of Antarctica, where the land is permanently covered by ice and snow.

- Deserts cover about one seventh of the Earth's surface.

147

NORTH AMERICA

The continent of North America stretches all the way from the frozen waters of the Arctic Ocean down to the warm Caribbean Sea. Most of its land is taken up by two huge countries, Canada and the United States of America. They both have vast areas of land, called national parks, which are protected for their beauty and wildlife. The famous Rocky Mountains run almost all the way down the western side of the continent.

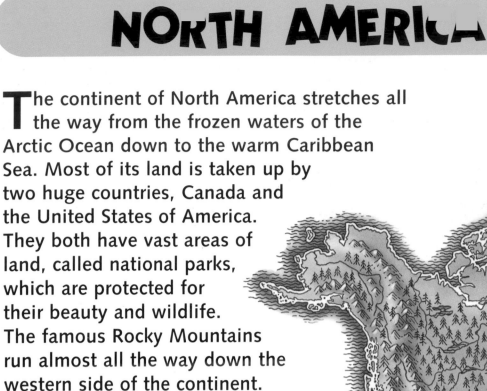

Factfile

- The Trans-Canada Highway stretches right across Canada for about 8,000 km.

- Lake *Superior* is the largest freshwater lake in the world.

- The famous Niagara Falls have two main waterfalls: the 49 m high Horseshoe Falls are in Canada; and the 51 m high American Falls are in the USA.

- The city of Chicago got its name from a Native American word for "place where wild onions grow".

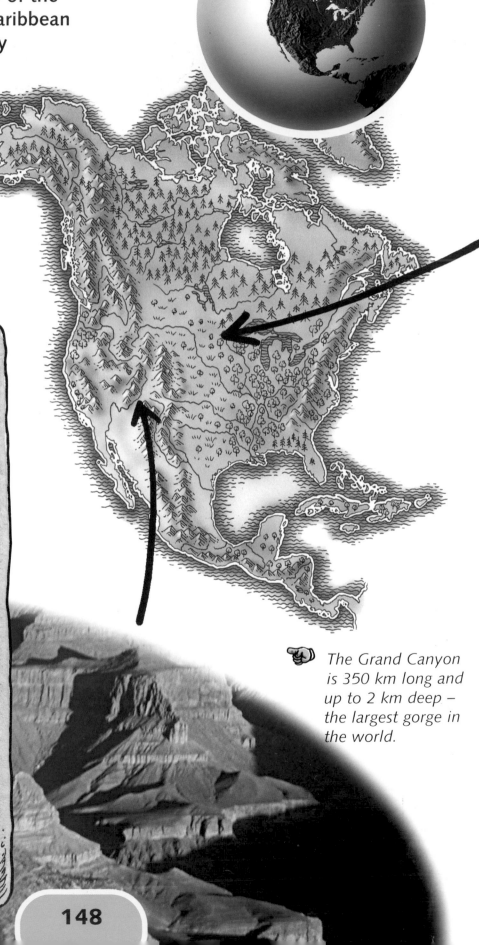

The Grand Canyon is 350 km long and up to 2 km deep – the largest gorge in the world.

☞ Prairies are large areas of flat grassland in Canada and the USA.

Quiz

1 In which American state is the Grand Canyon – Arizona, Florida or Wisconsin?

2 Which is the biggest of the Great Lakes?

3 What is the capital of the USA?

4 Which river flows over the Niagara Falls?

5 What is the name of the canal that joins the Pacific and Atlantic Oceans?

6 Canada is bigger than the USA – true or false?

Answers
1 Arizona, 2 Lake Superior 3 Washington DC,
4 Niagara River, 5 Panama Canal.
6 True.

THE ELEVATOR'S BROKEN DOWN!

Make a teepee

LARGE STRAWS

1. You'll need four cut-off garden sticks or large straws for the poles (about 20 cm long). Tie each set of two sticks in the form of an X, but with the cross-over point close to the top. Place one X over the other so that the cross-over points rest on each other. Bind the two together.

2. For the teepee shape draw a circle around a 20 cm wide plate on card, cut it out and then cut it in half. Paint your own pattern and cut out two door-holes.

3. Put the painted teepee shape round the sticks and close it with sticky tape or a card tab. Trim the sticks level with the bottom of the teepee.

We believe that the first people to set foot on the continent of North America were hunters from Northeast Asia. Many thousands of years ago they crossed a land bridge to the region that is now called Alaska. These native Americans gradually moved from the cold north to the warm south, settling the whole of the continent. It was less than 500 years ago that Europeans sailed across the Atlantic Ocean and made their own permanent settlements in what they called the New World.

Factfile

- The Inuit live in northern Canada and Greenland; they have their own homeland in Canada, called Nunavut (meaning "Our Land").

- The CN Tower in Toronto, Canada, is the world's tallest free-standing structure; it is 553 m high.

- The largest cities on the continent are New York, Mexico City and Los Angeles.

- The Aztecs of Mexico had their capital at Tenochtitlan; it was destroyed by Spanish conquerors in 1521 and Mexico City was built on top of the ruins.

This stepped pyramid temple was found at the Mayan city of Chichen Itza, in Mexico. The Mayan civilization flourished in Mexico, Guatemala and Belize from about AD300 to 900.

Cowboys ride bucking broncos at festivals of horsemanship called rodeos. The cowboy tries to stay on for as long as he can.

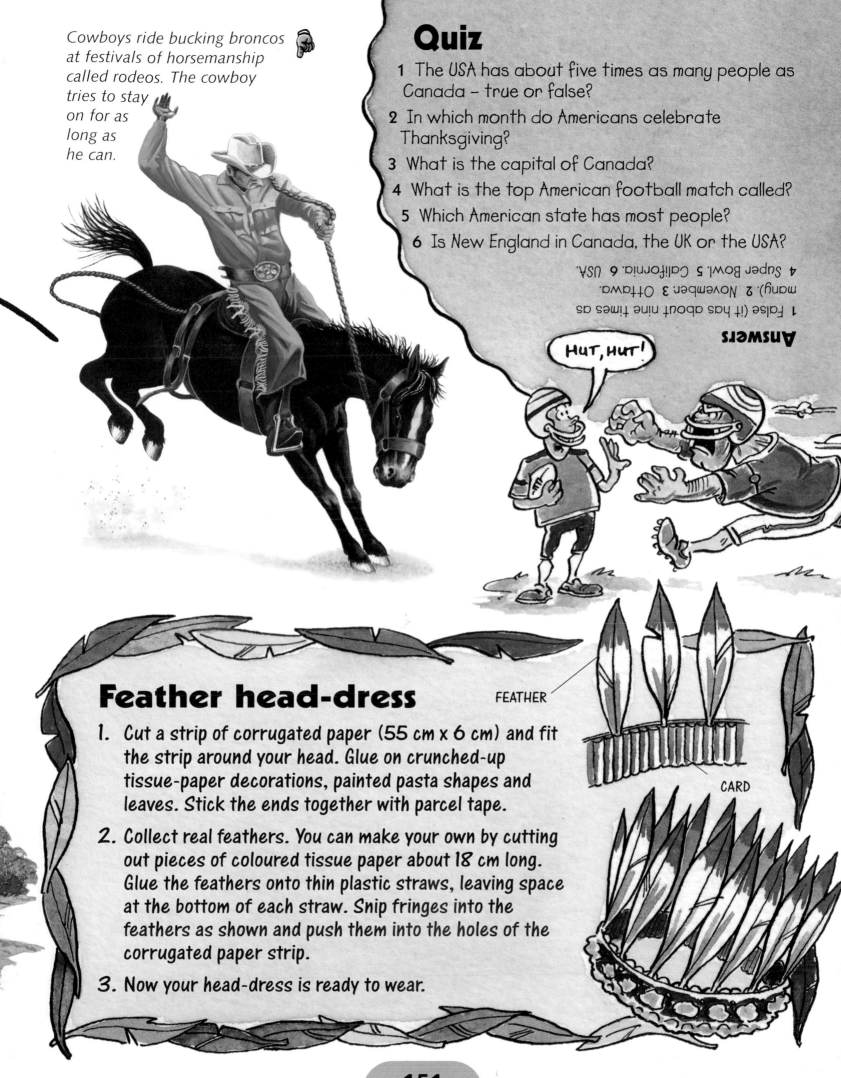

Quiz

1 The USA has about five times as many people as Canada – true or false?
2 In which month do Americans celebrate Thanksgiving?
3 What is the capital of Canada?
4 What is the top American football match called?
5 Which American state has most people?
6 Is New England in Canada, the UK or the USA?

Answers
1 False (it has about nine times as many). 2 November 3 Ottawa. 4 Super Bowl. 5 California. 6 USA.

HUT, HUT!

Feather head-dress

FEATHER

CARD

1. Cut a strip of corrugated paper (55 cm x 6 cm) and fit the strip around your head. Glue on crunched-up tissue-paper decorations, painted pasta shapes and leaves. Stick the ends together with parcel tape.

2. Collect real feathers. You can make your own by cutting out pieces of coloured tissue paper about 18 cm long. Glue the feathers onto thin plastic straws, leaving space at the bottom of each straw. Snip fringes into the feathers as shown and push them into the holes of the corrugated paper strip.

3. Now your head-dress is ready to wear.

SOUTH AMERICA

Brazil is by far the largest of the 13 countries that make up South America. It covers nearly half the continent's area. The world's longest range of mountains, the Andes, stretch down the western side of the continent. The River Amazon rises high up in the Andes of Peru. It flows for about 6,500 km through the world's largest rainforest, on its way to the Atlantic Ocean.

The Angel Falls, in Venezuela, form the world's highest waterfall. They plunge 979 m.

Quiz

1 Which is longer, the Andes mountain range or the Amazon river?

2 Which cape is at the southern tip of South America?

3 Which South American country is the world's largest producer of coffee?

4 Which is the smallest South American country?

5 What is the capital of Uruguay?

6 Which big cat lives in the Amazon rainforest?

MIAOW!

Answers
1 Andes. 2 Cape Horn.
3 Brazil. 4 Surinam.
5 Montevideo. 6 Jaguar.

152

Factfile

- There are more than 2,000 kinds of fish in the Amazon, including the deadly piranha.

- The Atacama Desert stretches for almost 1,000 km along the Pacific coast of Chile; the desert is very rich in minerals.

- The Amazon rainforest covers about six million sq km across parts of nine countries.

- The name Brazil comes from the Portuguese for "red wood dye".

- The world's largest open-cast copper mine is in Chile; the giant hole in the ground measures 4.8 km by 2.5 km.

More than one fifth of all the water in the world's rivers flows down the Amazon.

Watch out, there's an anaconda about

1. For a big anaconda cut the leg from an old pair of tights; for a baby anaconda use a long sock.

2. Stuff tights and socks with crumpled-up newspaper or scraps of fabric. Knot the end and cut it off next to the knot.

3. Stick or sew on buttons for eyes, make a mouth and a long forked tongue from card or material. Glue a nice smile on the baby.

4. Paint snake markings on your anacondas.

5. Make lots of snakes and wrap them around the furniture or even around yourself - they are quite harmless!

ATACAMA DESERT: WORLD'S DRIEST PLACE

Native American cultures had flourished for thousands of years when the first Europeans arrived in South America in the 1500s. Most of today's South Americans are descended from native Americans and Europeans, and many are a mixture of the two. Spanish is the continent's main language, except in Brazil, where people speak Portuguese. Native Americans still speak hundreds of Indian languages.

Gauchos herd cattle, making Argentina one of the world's biggest beef producers.

Factfile

- Lake Titicaca is the highest navigable lake in the world, at 3,811 m above sea level.

- Soccer is the most popular sport in South America; Brazil has won the World Cup four times.

- The mighty Inca empire once ruled over the Andes region from their capital city of Cuzco, in Peru.

- The Yanomami are the largest Amazonian forest tribe, but there are only about 19,000 of them left.

THIS IS EASY WITHOUT A GOALKEEPER!

Aymara people build reed boats to sail on Lake Titicaca, between Peru and Bolivia.

Rio carnival shakers

1. All you need is four yoghurt pots, dried peas and beans, some masking tape, sweet wrappers and coloured foil or paper for decoration.

2. Put the beans into one pot, then join it together with another pot using masking tape.

3. Glue on the sweet wrappers or cut-up pieces of coloured paper and foil.

4. Make another shaker in the same way and fill it with the peas to vary the sound.

5. Hold one in each hand and shake away!

EUROPE

Europe has a mainly rugged coastline that is dotted with islands. The northern parts of the continent are normally quite cold. They include a large region called Scandinavia, which is made up of Norway, Sweden, Finland, Denmark and the northern Atlantic island of Iceland. The central parts of Europe are milder, while the southern regions that lie around the Mediterranean Sea are mainly warm and dry.

The Tower of London was first built in 1078. Today it contains the British Crown Jewels.

Factfile

- The Eiffel Tower was completed in 1889; it is 300 m high and was the tallest building in the world until 1930.

- Iceland is called an island of fire and ice, because it is normally very cold but has active volcanoes and hot springs.

- The part of Russia to the west of the Ural Mountains, including Moscow and St Petersburg, is in Europe.

- The largest country in Europe (excluding Russia) is the Ukraine, with an area of 603,700 sq km.

- The most populated European country is Germany (with 82,190,000 people).

The Eiffel Tower is the most famous landmark of Paris, the capital of France.

Build a junk town

1. Collect together lots of small cardboard boxes for your houses. Cereal packets make good skyscrapers. Use a large cardboard lid or piece of card for the base.

2. Mark out roads, a park and spaces for your houses with a pencil. Paint the roads grey and the park and gardens green. Paint the boxes to look like houses with doors and windows. Cut some card to make the roofs. Stick together a number of small boxes to make blocks of flats, a supermarket, a school and a church. Arrange all the houses on the base. Make some trees from twigs stuck in plasticine.

Quiz

1 Which continent is the non-European part of Russia in?

2 The Black Sea's water is black – true or false?

3 Which is larger, Norway or Sweden?

4 In which city are the ancient Forum and Colosseum?

5 Which sea's name means "in the middle of the earth"?

6 Which three countries make up Benelux?

OH, NO!!

Answers
1 Asia. 2 False (it's greeny blue).
3 Sweden. 4 Rome.
5 Mediterranean. 6 Belgium, the Netherlands and Luxembourg.

Europe is full of many small countries and different peoples. Most have different cultures and customs, but they also have a lot in common. The northern Scandinavians are descendants of the Vikings. Further south, the French, Spanish and Italian languages all came from Latin, the language of the ancient Romans. Ancient Greek and Roman civilizations influenced European ideas of art, philosophy and law.

☞ *Flamenco is a traditional way of dancing and singing to guitar music that is very popular in Spain.*

Make a Spanish fan

1. Take a long sheet of paper and paint a bright pattern on it. Then decorate it with glitter glue.

2. When it's dry, fold the sheet into a concertina, keeping the folds all the same size. Staple the folds together at one end and attach this to a lolly stick for a handle.

3. Now you can keep cool with your fancy Spanish fan.

During the winter months, the Alps attracts millions of visitors. The largest mountain range in Europe, it extends through France, Italy, Switzerland and Austria.

Quiz

1 Which famous church leader lives in the Vatican City, in Rome?

2 In which country is the ancient stone circle called Stonehenge?

3 Which is bigger, France or Spain?

4 What is the name of the pleated skirt worn by Scotsmen?

5 In which country do some people speak Catalan?

6 What is the capital of the Czech Republic?

Answers

1 The Pope. 2 UK. 3 France. 4 Kilt 5 Spain. 6 Prague.

Factfile

• Venice is built on more than 100 islands in a lagoon; it has 177 canals.

• Vatican City, in Rome, is the world's smallest country, with an area of 0.44 sq. km.

• Finland has more than 60,000 lakes; its Finnish name, Suomi, means "land of lakes and marshes".

• The Baltic states of Lithuania, Latvia and Estonia were part of the former Soviet Union until 1991, when they regained their independence.

ASIA

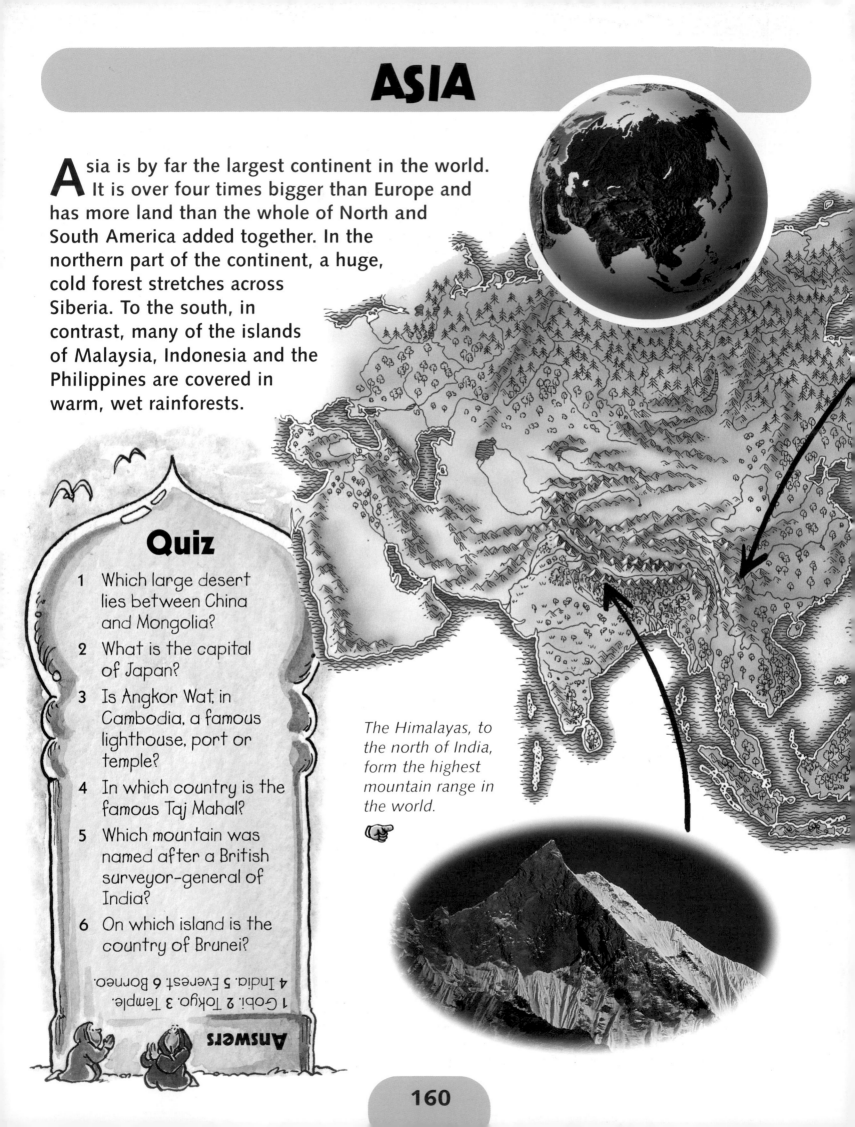

Asia is by far the largest continent in the world. It is over four times bigger than Europe and has more land than the whole of North and South America added together. In the northern part of the continent, a huge, cold forest stretches across Siberia. To the south, in contrast, many of the islands of Malaysia, Indonesia and the Philippines are covered in warm, wet rainforests.

Quiz

1 Which large desert lies between China and Mongolia?

2 What is the capital of Japan?

3 Is Angkor Wat, in Cambodia, a famous lighthouse, port or temple?

4 In which country is the famous Taj Mahal?

5 Which mountain was named after a British surveyor-general of India?

6 On which island is the country of Brunei?

Answers
1 Gobi. 2 Tokyo. 3 Temple. 4 India. 5 Everest 6 Borneo.

The Himalayas, to the north of India, form the highest mountain range in the world.

The Great Wall of China was first built over 2,000 years ago, to keep out invaders from the north.

JUST TRY TO CLEAN IT UP GRACEFULLY!

Factfile

- The Japanese tea ceremony has been handed down from ancient times, and is still used to show grace and good manners.

- Mount Everest, in the Himalayas, is the world's highest mountain, at 8,848 m.

- Altogether, the Great Wall of China is about 6,400 km long; it used to be said that it could be seen from the Moon but lunar astronauts disagree.

- Japan's most famous mountain, Fuji, is a sacred volcano that last erupted in 1707.

Japanese flower arrangement

1. It's easy to make a simple arrangement in a see-through bowl.

2. Put soil at the bottom of the bowl, and add gravel, shells and pebbles. Now push a small twig through the gravel into the soil.

3. Half-fill the bowl with water and decorate the surface with pretty leaves and flowers (real or paper).

This is simple Asian beauty.

ASIAN PEOPLE

The world's first civilizations grew up in Southwest Asia. Early wandering people first settled in the fertile region between two great rivers, the Euphrates and the Tigris. They started to grow crops and eventually built cities. Today, more than half the world's people live in Asia. This continent also includes the country with more people than any other, China. This was an important and powerful empire in ancient times.

Factfile

• The first people to climb Mount Everest were a Nepalese Sherpa called Tenzing Norgay and a New Zealander named Edmund Hillary, in 1953.

• Sherpa people live in some of the highest villages in the world, in the Himalayas. They are farmers and herders, as well as skilled mountaineers.

• The Sultan of Brunei, one of the world's richest men, has a palace with 1,788 rooms.

• The Petronas Towers in Kuala Lumpur, the capital of Malaysia, form the world's tallest building; the twin towers are 452 m high.

Floating markets in Thailand make it easy to transport produce.

Weave a Persian rug

Ancient Persians made the most beautiful rugs, now you can too!

1. Fold 12 double-pages of newspaper into strips. Fold each sheet in half lengthways, then fold it in half twice more and press each strip to flatten it out.

2. Place six strips side by side to form an even edge, and tape them down so they stay in position. Weave the other six strips over and under the strips you taped down, as shown. The first, third and fifth strips go over and under.

The second, fourth and sixth strips go under and over.

3. Untape the strips and push the rows together, moving the strips until the ends are even all around the rug. Fold the loose ends of the strips over and tuck them in.

PAPER STRIPS

Japanese sumo wrestlers are big and very strong. They try to throw their opponent down or force him out of the ring.

I THINK I'M GOING TO NEED A LONGER LADDER!

Petronas Towers

Quiz

1. How many islands make up the Philippines, 7, 70, 700 or 7,000?
2. What is the capital of Thailand?
3. Chinese New Year is on 1 January – true or false?
4. Which country does the island of Honshu belong to?
5. Which country was named after King Philip II of Spain?
6. Which country does Hong Kong belong to?

Answers

1 700.0. 2 Bangkok.
3 False (it's between 21 January and 20 February). 4 Japan.
5 Philippines. 6 China.

AFRICA

Africa lies across the equator. It is the second largest continent and makes up a fifth of the world's land area. It is made up of 53 countries, some very large and others very small. There are vast areas of unspoilt wilderness across Africa, and the Sahara Desert covers more than a quarter of the continent. Huge stretches of savannah grassland are home to giraffes, rhinos and lions, and elephants roam the bush.

Factfile

- Camels store fat in their humps and can go for a long time without water; they can travel as far as 160 km across the desert in a day.

- The Victoria Falls plunge over a drop of 108 m on the Zambezi River, on the border between Zambia and Zimbabwe.

- Africa's highest mountain, Kilimanjaro, rises to 5,895 m in Tanzania.

- Lake Victoria (69,500 sq km) is Africa's largest lake; Lake Volta (8,482 sq km), in Ghana, is the world's largest artificial lake.

The stone ruins of Great Zimbabwe once enclosed many mud buildings. The oldest parts date from the 700s.

Bake a dough desert

1. Mix smooth dough from six cups of flour, three cups of salt, six tablespoons of cooking oil and water. Roll the dough out, shape it into desert dunes, and then ask an adult to bake it at the bottom of the oven at a low temperature for 40 minutes.

2. When it is cool, paint with PVA glue and sprinkle with real sand. Paint a green oasis, then paint pipe-cleaners green and make them into palm trees. Plant them in lumps of plasticine on the oasis.

Camels are still used by some traders to transport goods across the Sahara desert in North Africa.

Quiz

1. Which country is the world's biggest gold producer?
2. One branch of the Nile is called Blue Nile – what is the other called?
3. What is the cape at the southern tip of Africa called?
4. What is the largest country in Africa?
5. Which is Egypt's (and Africa's) largest city?
6. Niger is an African country; name another by adding two letters.

Answers
1 South Africa.
2 White Nile. 3 Cape of Good Hope. 4 Sudan.
5 Cairo. 6 Nigeria.

SAY CHEESE!

165

AFRICAN PEOPLE

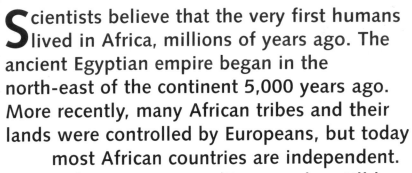

Scientists believe that the very first humans lived in Africa, millions of years ago. The ancient Egyptian empire began in the north-east of the continent 5,000 years ago. More recently, many African tribes and their lands were controlled by Europeans, but today most African countries are independent. The continent's native peoples still have their own cultures and languages. They traditionally lived in villages and farmed the land, but today there are many growing cities.

 The beaded necklace and headdress is traditional for the Masai tribes of Kenya and Tanzania.

Quiz

1 Which is South Africa's largest city?

2 What is the name of the desert in Namibia?

3 Which African country has the largest population?

4 How many times does the winding River Congo cross the equator?

5 Which famous flat-topped mountain overlooks the city of Cape Town?

6 Does Africa have a larger population than China?

Answers
1 Johannesburg. 2 Namib.
3 Nigeria. 4 Twice.
5 Table Mountain. 6 No.

Johannesburg is the largest city in South Africa with a population of about four million.

Factfile

- Ostriches are the world's biggest birds and the fastest on land, growing up to 2.5 m tall and running at up to 65 km/h.

- The Suez Canal, in Egypt, is 169 km long; it was opened in 1869 to join the Mediterranean and Red Seas.

- The Mbuti pygmies of central Africa are the world's shortest people; some women are just 1.24 m tall.

- About half a million people live as nomads around the Sahara Desert.

- The Skeleton Coast of Namibia was named because of the many shipwrecks on its shores.

Papier-mâché African bangle

1. Cut a cardboard strip about 28 cm long and 3 cm wide. Overlap the ends to fit loosely over the wrist, allowing for the added papier mâché, and tape them together.

2. Mix some PVA glue with water until you have a paste. Tear newspaper into small strips, dip them into the paste and wrap them around the bangle. Cover it with three paper layers. When the papier mâché is dry (it might take a few days), paint the bangle with white paint and then add your own African patterns.

3. For extra effect you could varnish your bangle with clear gloss enamel.

NEWSPAPER STRIPS

GOOD JOB OSTRICHES CAN'T FLY!

AUSTRALASIA

This continent is made up of Australia, New Zealand, Papua New Guinea and thousands of small islands in the South Pacific Ocean. The region is sometimes called Oceania. Australia is much bigger than all the other countries put together. It is a warm, dry country, and much of its land is desert and dry bush, called outback. New Zealand has a milder climate. The warm Pacific Islands cover a vast area, but most of them are very small with few people.

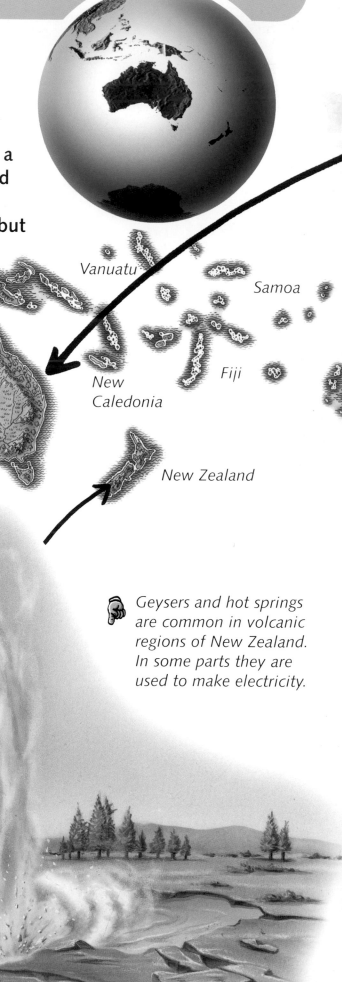

Vanuatu

Samoa

Australia

New Caledonia

Fiji

New Zealand

Geysers and hot springs are common in volcanic regions of New Zealand. In some parts they are used to make electricity.

Factfile

- The roofs of the *Sydney Opera House* (which opened in 1973) were designed to look like giant sails.

- The Great Barrier Reef is made up of over 2,000 individual coral reefs spread along 2,100 km.

- Sydney was founded in 1788, when the first European settlers arrived in Australia.

- Many Aboriginal rock paintings are thousands of years old. They tell ancient stories.

The Great Barrier Reef lies just off the coast of northeast Australia and is home to a huge variety of fish and other marine life.

Quiz

1 Which town lies right in the middle of Australia?

2 Are there sharks at the Great Barrier Reef?

3 Where do kiwis live?

4 Which is biggest, Fiji, Samoa or Tonga?

5 Are corals plants or animals?

6 The biggest desert in Australia is called the Great Sandy Desert – true or false.

Answers
1 Alice Springs. 2 Yes. 3 New Zealand. 4 Fiji. 5 Animals. 6 True.

Aboriginal rock painting

1. Collect some interesting stones and paint them with poster paint. Look at the shape of the stones and make them into crocodiles, fish, birds, kangaroos, flowers, plants and strange creatures. Always wait for the paint to dry before adding another colour. When you've painted an interesting animal you could glue on pipe cleaners for tails, feelers or legs.

2. The Aborigines paint their dreams. Paint your best dream on a stone – it could be a ship that will take you down under to Australia.

WATCH OUT, OR YOU'LL BREAK THE WINDOWS IN THE OPERA HOUSE!

AUSTRALASIAN PEOPLE

The first Australians were Aborigines, who came from Asia about 40,000 years ago. They probably crossed land that is now under water. The first New Zealanders were Maoris, who sailed from the Polynesian islands in about AD800. According to Maori legend, they arrived in just seven canoes. The Pacific islanders themselves sailed from Southeast Asia about 5,000 years ago. In Australia and New Zealand most of the modern inhabitants are descended from European settlers.

Uluru, or Ayers Rock, is a sacred place to the Aborigines. In 1985 it was returned to them to run as a national park with the Australian government.

Quiz

1   Can you go swimming in Lake Eyre?

2   What is the nickname of the Australian rugby union team?

3   Where is the famous Harbour Bridge?

4   On which island does Papua New Guinea lie?

5   What is the capital of Australia?

6   Which country do the Cook Islands belong to?

Answers
1 No (it's normally dry) 2 Wallabies 3 Sydney. 4 New Guinea. 5 Canberra. 6 New Zealand.

Wood carving is a traditional craft of the Maoris of New Zealand; they decorate their meeting houses with carvings.

Factfile

- The giant rock of Uluru rises 348 m above the desert plain in central Australia.

- Australia is the sixth biggest country in the world, but only just over 18 million people live there.

- New Zealand's capital, Wellington, is the southern-most capital city in the world.

- The didgeridoo is a long, hollow, wooden pipe played by Aborigines.

- There are three main groups of Pacific islands: Micronesia ("small islands"), Melanesia ("black islands") and Polynesia ("many islands").

HE HASN'T REALISED THE MUSIC HAS STOPPED!

Make a didgeridoo pipe

1. Poke holes into one side of a long cardboard tube (from kitchen roll, for example). Now paint the tube.

2. When it's dry, cover one end with greaseproof paper and hold it in place with a rubber band.

3. To play your pipe, hum into the open end and move your fingers over the holes to make different sounds.

GREASEPROOF PAPER

ELASTIC BAND

ANTARCTICA

The frozen continent of Antarctica lies around the South Pole, at the very bottom of the Earth. The land is covered by a giant icecap, and beneath the ice there are mountains and valleys. No one lives permanently in Antarctica, but there are several bases where scientists work. In winter, temperatures drop to -50°C and there are fierce, freezing winds.

Factfile

- Norwegian explorer Roald Amundsen and his team were the first people to reach the South Pole, in 1911.

- The Transantarctic Mountains stretch for 3,500 km across the entire continent.

- Antarctica means "opposite the Arctic".

- The highest Antarctic mountain is Vinson Massif (5,140 m).

- 90 percent of an iceberg's mass is below the surface of the sea.

Penguins nest in huge colonies called rookeries. They come to land to breed but spend most of their time at sea.

The Amundsen-Scott station stands at the South Pole; a dome protects the buildings inside.

THE UNITED STATES OF AMERICA
WELCOMES YOU TO
AMUNDSEN - SCOTT SOUTH POLE STATION

Quiz

1 Which British explorer was second to reach the South Pole?

2 Do polar bears live in Antarctica?

3 The Ross Ice Shelf is about the size of France – true or false?

4 Which are bigger, emperor penguins or king penguins?

5 What is the name of the imaginary line around the region of Antarctica?

6 Is Antarctica's Mount Erebus a dormant volcano?

Answers
1 Robert Scott 2 No 3 True.
4 Emperor penguins. 5 Antarctic
Circle. 6 No (it's active).

Ice-cream iceberg

1. Next time you have a party, you could explore the polar regions with your friends.

2. Get a big tub of vanilla ice-cream and stack scoops of ice-cream on a large white plate or tray. Shape the ice-cream into icebergs and ice shelves and sprinkle on coconut. Make a glacier shape with a fork. You could add some ice cubes too.

3. Now give out spoons and get stuck into Antarctica.

EVERYWHERE I LOOK IS NORTH!

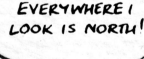

SOUTH POLE

ANCIENT EGYPT

Over 5,000 years ago, people settled near the River Nile, in north-east Africa. The ancient Egyptians farmed the fertile land beside their great river. They were ruled by a king, called a pharaoh. They believed that their hawk-god, Horus, entered a new pharaoh and made him a god too. The Egyptians believed in life after death, and pharaohs were buried with things they wanted to take to the next world.

Egyptian queen with two noblewomen.

The Great Pyramid at Giza (one of three large pyramids there) is the only one of the Seven Wonders of the Ancient World still standing.

Hundreds of beautiful golden objects were found in the tomb of the boy-pharaoh Tutankhamun in the Valley of the Kings.

Factfile

- The Great Pyramid is 147 m high; each side of its square base is 230 m long.

- It took about 100,000 men over 20 years to build the Great Pyramid, using more than two million heavy blocks of stone.

- The Egyptians preserved dead bodies by covering them with salt crystals called natron and wrapping them in linen bandages.

- Cats were sacred to the ancient Egyptians, and they worshipped a cat-goddess named Bast.

Quiz

1 Which sea does the River Nile flow into?

2 How old was Tutankhamun when he died – 18, 28 or 38?

3 What is the capital of modern Egypt?

4 How tall is the Great Sphinx – 2, 20 or 200 m?

5 What was the name of the Egyptian reed that was used for writing on?

6 The ancient Egyptians were fond of beer – true or false?

Answers

1 Mediterranean. 2 18. 3 Cairo.
4 20 m. 5 Papyrus. 6 True.

DO YOU THINK THE GREAT SPHINX IS A LION WITH A MAN'S HEAD OR A MAN WITH A LION'S BODY?

Write your name in hieroglyphs

1. The ancient Egyptians invented a system of writing using picture symbols, called hieroglyphs.

2. Use this alphabet to write your own name in hieroglyphs.

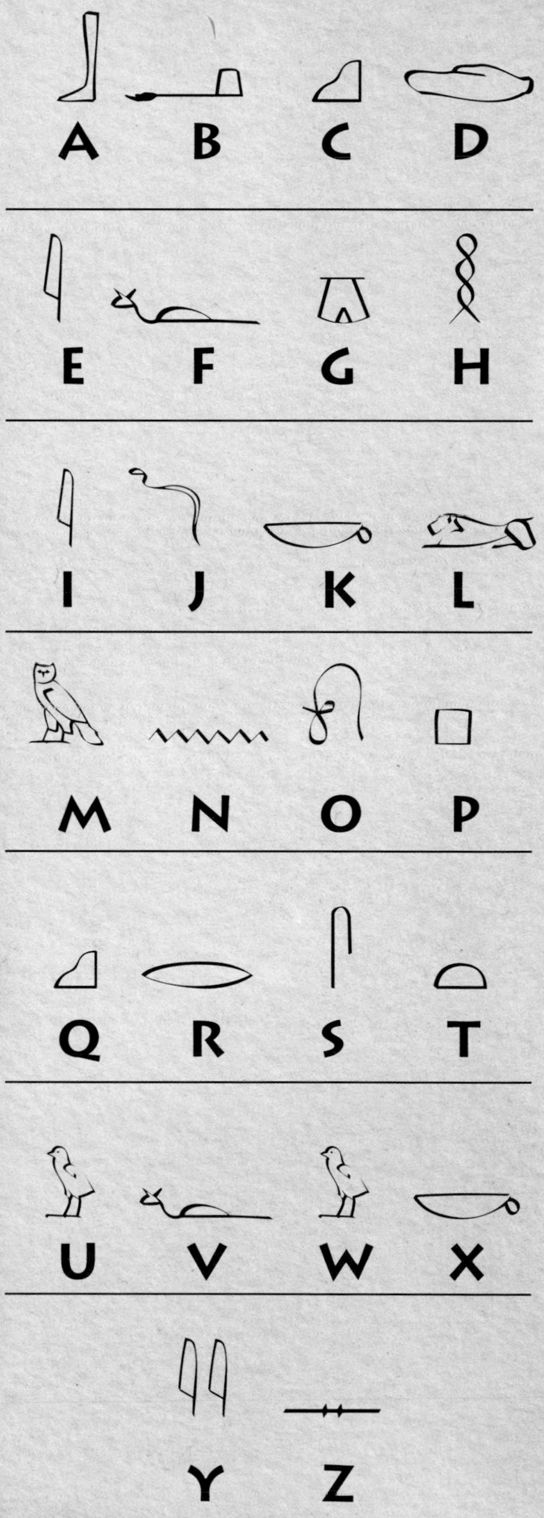

A B C D

E F G H

I J K L

M N O P

Q R S T

U V W X

Y Z

ANCIENT GREECE

Around 800BC a new civilization developed in Greece. The ancient Greeks produced many fine buildings and built important cities. They wrote great plays and Greek philosophers, or "lovers of wisdom", thought about and discussed important problems and ideas.

👆 Greek king with his attendants.

👆 The ancient Greeks built the world's first theatres, which were made of stone and built into hillsides.

Quiz

1 Who was the messenger of the Greek gods?
2 Which ancient city is the capital of modern Greece?
3 How many banks of rowers were on each side of a bireme?
4 Which famous temple stands on the Acropolis in Athens?
5 Who was not a philosopher – Plato, Hades, Aristotle?
6 Demeter was the goddess of rain – true or false?

Answers
1 Hermes. 2 Athens. 3 Two. 4 Parthenon.
5 Hades (he was god of the dead).
6 False (she was goddess of grain).

176

Greek drama mask

1. Cut out a piece of card bigger than your face. Draw on and cut out large eye holes. For a nose fold a piece of card, cut it to shape and glue it on.

2. Cut pieces out of old tights to fit over the eye holes, so people can't see you but you can see them, and glue them into position. Paint the mask white, outline the eyes with black paint and add a happy or a sad mouth. Cut strips of paper for hair and stick them on at the back. Attach a stick to the back of the mask and secure it with parcel tape.

3. Now hold up your mask and face the audience.

Greek warships called triremes had three banks of rowers on each side and were used to ram and sink enemy ships.

Factfile

- The first ancient Olympic Games were held in 776BC at Olympia, a site dedicated to the god Zeus.

- Ancient Greek athletes sometimes carried shields and wore helmets, but no clothes!

- Zeus was king of the Greek gods, and his wife was called Hera.

- In the city state of Sparta, boys were trained to fight from the age of seven.

ANCIENT ROME

The city of Rome began as a small village on one of a group of seven hills, over 2,700 years ago. When the village grew into a city, the Romans conquered other peoples in Italy. Then the Roman army marched further afield to create an empire that stretched around the Mediterranean Sea and as far north as Britain.

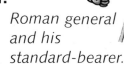

Roman general and his standard-bearer.

Roman soldiers built thousands of kilometres of straight roads throughout their empire, and some Roman roads still exist today.

Factfile

- According to legend, Rome was founded in 753BC by two twins, Romulus and Remus, who were raised by a she-wolf.

- Rome was first governed by kings, then it became a republic. Its first emperor, Augustus, took office in 27BC.

- Most Roman gladiators were slaves who had been captured in war.

- The Colosseum in Rome was completed in AD80. It could hold about 50,000 spectators.

Gladiators fought to the death for the amusement of the huge crowds. Other shows included men fighting against animals such as lions, rhinos and bears.

BE GENTLE!

Quiz

1 What do we call the structures that brought water into Roman cities?

2 What was the name of the main square in ancient Rome?

3 What was a Roman officer who commanded 100 soldiers called?

4 Which famous Roman was murdered on the Ides of March?

5 Which Roman emperor built a wall to keep Scottish tribes out?

6 Did Asterix and Obelix really exist?

Answers
1 Aqueducts. 2 The Forum.
3 Centurion. 4 Julius
Caesar 5 Hadrian. 6 No.

The Italian town of Pompeii was buried under volcanic ash when nearby Mount Vesuvius erupted in AD79.

Match the Roman soldiers

Roman soldiers wore different uniforms and carried different weapons according to their rank and the sort of fighting they did.

Can you spot which two in the row of soldiers below are exactly the same?

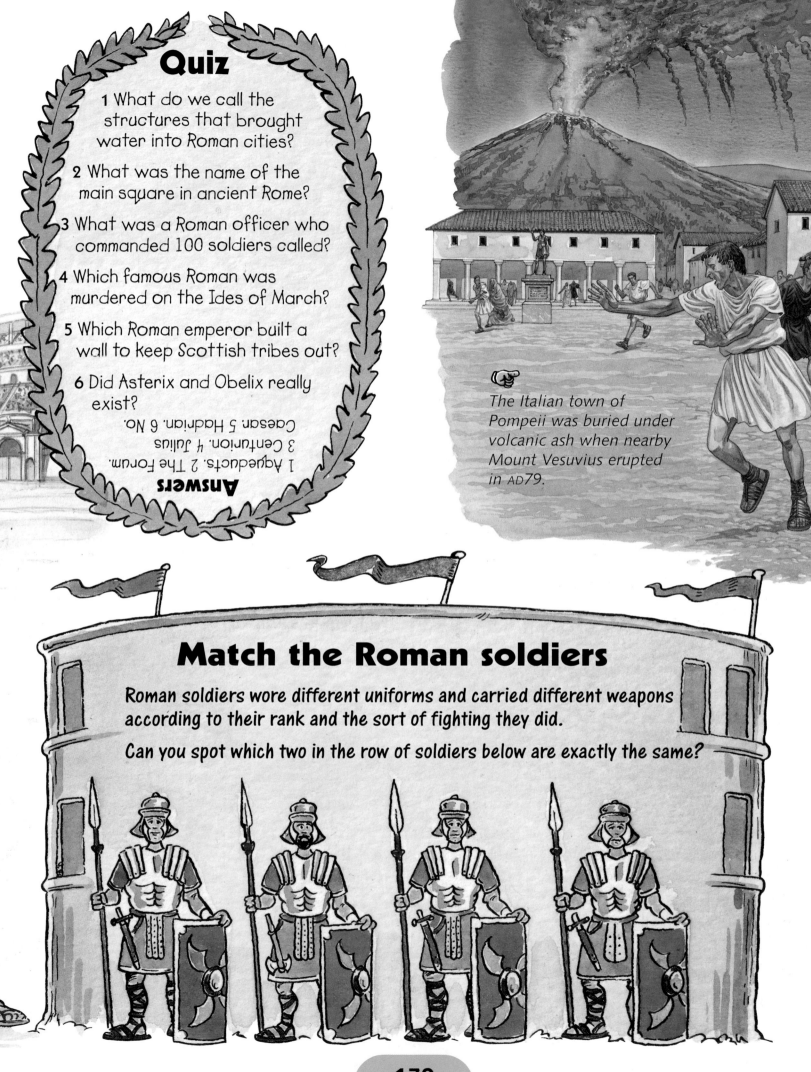

THE MIDDLE AGES

The Middle Ages is the name usually given to a period of history that started in about AD500 and lasted for around a thousand years. We think of the period before the Middle Ages as ancient history, and afterwards as modern times. During the Middle Ages European countries were ruled by kings and emperors who generally owned the land. They divided it among their most important men, called nobles. The nobles were supported by knights, who were trained to fight. Peasants farmed the land, growing food for their families and their lord.

Henry VI and VII with members of the Court.

Medieval kings and nobles built castles to protect themselves from enemies.

Quiz

1 What were mechanical bows that shot bolts called?

2 What was tapped on a squire's shoulder to make him a knight?

3 What was the name of a medieval entertainer who clowned around?

4 Which famous city did the Crusaders conquer in 1099?

5 What was the water surrounding a castle called?

6 Which weapon did knights use for jousting?

1 Crossbows. 2 Sword. 3 Jester. 4 Jerusalem. 5 Moat 6 Lance.
Answers

Factfile

- In medieval towns there were no proper drains, so people threw their rubbish and emptied their pots into the street.

- A terrible plague called the Black Death spread from Asia to Europe in the 1300s and killed at least a third of the population.

- For a period of almost 200 years, from 1095, Christian knights went on Crusades to win back the Holy Land from Muslim rulers.

Knights often took part in tournaments, where they jousted with each other on horseback.

Make a stained-glass window

1. Draw a window frame on a piece of thick black paper and cut it out. You can make up your own frame and designs, but they should be big enough so that you can cut them out easily.

2. Place a sheet of tracing paper on the table, the same size as your window. Glue or tape the frame onto the decorated tracing paper and arrange small pieces of coloured tissue paper or cellophane on it. Apply tiny dabs of glue to stick on the coloured pieces.

3. Hang the stained glass up in your window and watch the colours light up when the sun shines through.

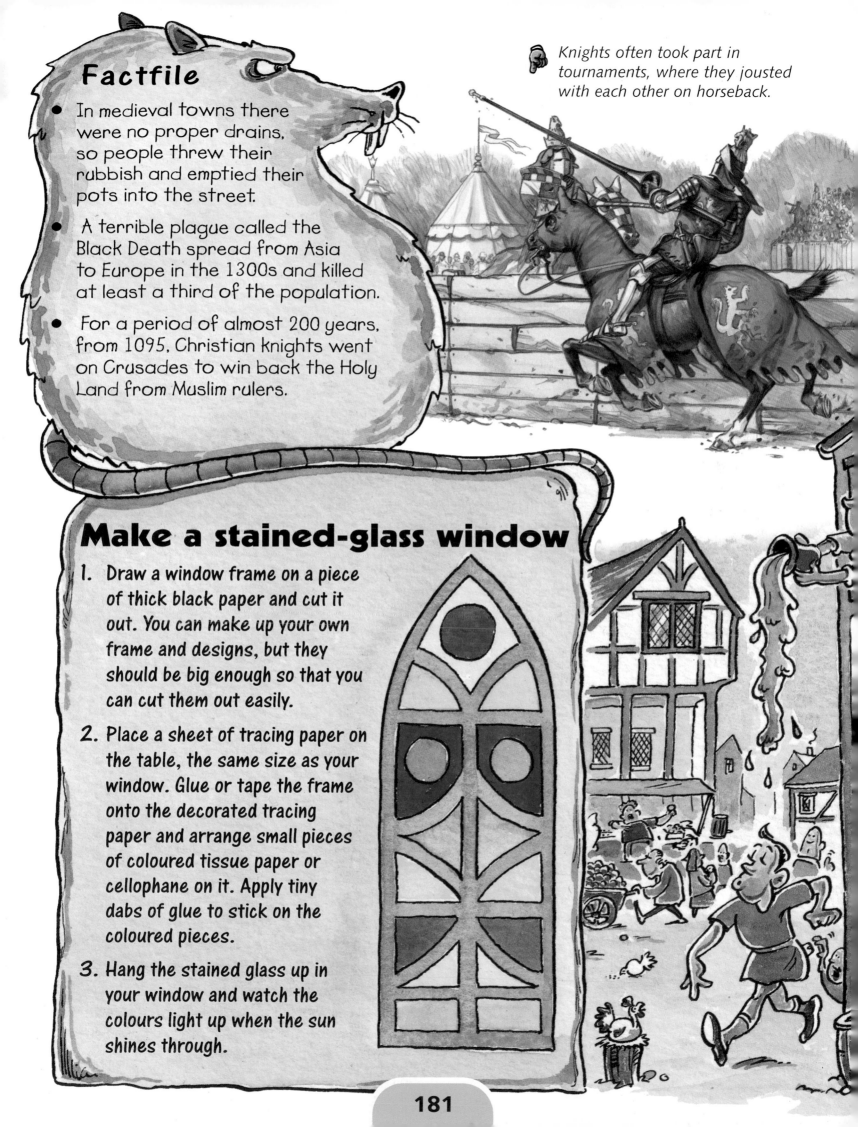

LANGUAGES OF THE WORLD

Language is made up of the words we speak or write down. Words help us to communicate with each other, to tell each other things. There are thousands of different languages all over the world, as well as different alphabets for writing them down. Most people grow up speaking just one language, called their mother tongue, but they often learn other foreign languages when they are older.

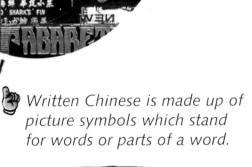

Say hello to over 1,400 million people!

There are about 4,000 different languages spoken in the world! This is how to write and say hello in just eight of them.

FRENCH

Hello - **Bonjour**
(bon - shoor)

ITALIAN

Hello - **Ciao**
(chow)

RUSSIAN

Hello - **Здравствуйте**
(zdras - vid - ye)

MANDARIN

Hello - 你好
(nee - how)

JAPANESE

Hello - こんにちは
(kon - nich - ee - wah)

HEBREW

Hello - שלום
(sha - lom)

ARABIC

Hello - أهلا
(eh - lun)

SWAHILI

Hello - **Jambo**
(jam - bow)

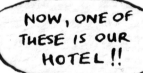

Written Chinese is made up of picture symbols which stand for words or parts of a word.

NOW, ONE OF THESE IS OUR HOTEL !!

It'll never catch on!

Quiz

1 What is the main language of Quebec, in Canada?

2 In which country is Urdu the official language?

3 What are the two main languages of Switzerland?

4 What do Italians call Rome?

5 Arabic is written from right to left – true or false?

6 What is the most frequently used letter in written English?

Answers
1 French. 2 Pakistan.
3 French and German.
4 Roma. 5 True. 6 E.

Factfile

● Mandarin Chinese is the most spoken language in the world, followed by English and Hindi (the main official language of India).

● Russian has its own alphabet, which came originally from Greek; it has 33 letters.

● The international flag code has a different flag for all 26 letters of the English alphabet, and is still sometimes used by sailors.

● Holy Roman Emperor Charles V (1500-58) is said to have spoken French to men, Italian to women, German to horses and Spanish to God.

● There are about 1,300 languages in Africa alone.

The Rosetta stone is an ancient carved stone slab that was discovered in 1799. It was used to decipher Egyptian hieroglyphics, which before then modern people could not understand.

183

RELIGIONS

Religion has been practised in different ways in all known civilizations from the earliest times. The world's main modern religions have existed for thousands of years, trying to explain the world and the meaning and purpose of life to their believers. It is thought that more than three-quarters of the world's people follow some form of religion. The religions and their followers have a lot in common.

Hindu gods and goddesses have been worshipped in India and neighbouring countries for thousands of years.

Factfile

- Jerusalem is a holy city for Muslims, Jews and Christians.

- Hinduism is a major religion in India and neighbouring countries; it is thousands of years old.

- Christianity has about 1,930 million followers; Islam about 1,100 million; Hinduism about 780 million; and Buddhism about 325 million.

- Shintoism, the ancient religion of Japan, has about 120 million followers.

- The Sikh religion began in India over 500 years ago; Sikhs follow the lessons of teachers called gurus.

I BRING FRANKINCENSE, BUT MUM SAYS CAN SHE HAVE THE JAR BACK!

Match the symbols to the religions

1. All religions have special symbols which mean a great deal to their followers.

2. Can you match these five symbols to the right religions? The answers are below.

1.

2.

3.

4.

5.

A. Hindu
B. Christian
C. Muslim
D. Buddhism
E. Shinto

Quiz

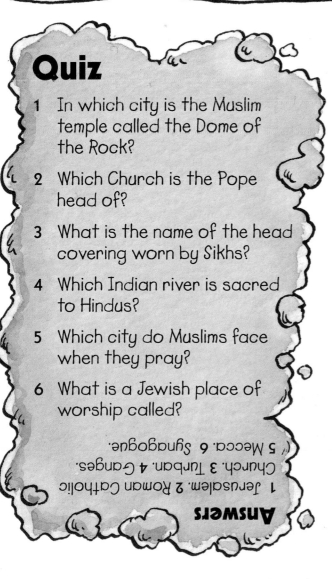

1 In which city is the Muslim temple called the Dome of the Rock?

2 Which Church is the Pope head of?

3 What is the name of the head covering worn by Sikhs?

4 Which Indian river is sacred to Hindus?

5 Which city do Muslims face when they pray?

6 What is a Jewish place of worship called?

Answers
1 Jerusalem. 2 Roman Catholic Church. 3 Turban. 4 Ganges. 5 Mecca. 6 Synagogue.

The Wailing Wall is a holy site for all Jews. It was part of the Temple of Jerusalem which was first built by King Solomon in 950BC. After being destroyed in 586BC, the Temple was re-built and again destroyed. The Wailing Wall is now part of the Muslim Dome of the Rock.

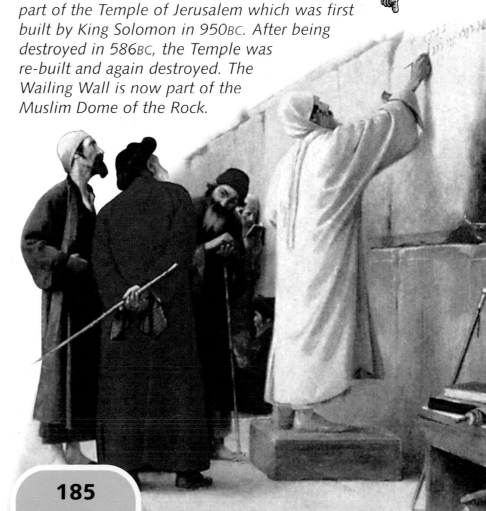

FESTIVALS AND CUSTOMS

There are thousands of different festivals all over the world. They mostly celebrate a person or an event, and many of them happen once a year on special days called holidays. Many holidays, or "holy days", are linked with religion, such as Christian Easter, Islamic Eid Al-Fittr and Hindu Holi. Many festivals and religions have given rise to special customs and traditions, which are kept alive by being handed down from one generation to the next.

Piñata game

The piñata is a Mexican toy full of goodies.

1. Stuff a paper bag with scrunched-up newspaper to make it firm, and then tie it with string. Paint and decorate the bag. Screw up pieces of tissue paper, cut strips of crêpe paper and paste them on. Untie the bag, take out the newspaper and fill it with sweets. Retie the string and ask an adult to hang your piñata from the ceiling.

2. Blindfold a player, give him or her a rolled-up newspaper and let them have a go at knocking down the piñata. Each player can have three attempts and then it's the next person's turn. When somebody knocks the piñata down, share the sweets out among everyone.

 Dragon dancers weave through the streets, celebrating Chinese New Year.

The annual carnival in Rio de Janeiro, Brazil, is the most famous in the world.

Factfile

- Halloween, celebrated on 31 October, is a shortening of All Hallows Eve, or "the day before the feast of All Saints".

- The Hindus of India and Nepal like to play tricks during their spring festival of Holi, such as throwing coloured powder and water at each other.

- In northern Europe people traditionally dance around the maypole on 1 May to celebrate the coming of spring.

- Some people think that the year 2000 is the last year of the old century and millennium rather than the first year of the new century and millennium.

SPORTS

People love taking part in sports because they are fun to play and give you good exercise at the same time. Sports are also exciting to watch, and people all over the world are brought together by their interest in top sporting events. The Olympic Games, both summer and winter, World Cup soccer, Wimbledon tennis, Tour de France cycling: all these world-famous events have a long and interesting history.

The winner of the men's 100 m at the Olympics is usually called the fastest man on Earth.

Quiz

1 How many events are there in the decathlon?

2 Do female gymnasts perform on the rings?

3 Which city do the Yankees baseball team come from?

4 What colour jersey does the Tour de France leader wear?

5 Which country has won most Olympic gold medals?

6 Which martial art means "kick-punch-method"?

SORRY!

Answers
1 Ten. 2 No.
3 New York. 4 Yellow.
5 USA. 6 Taekwondo.

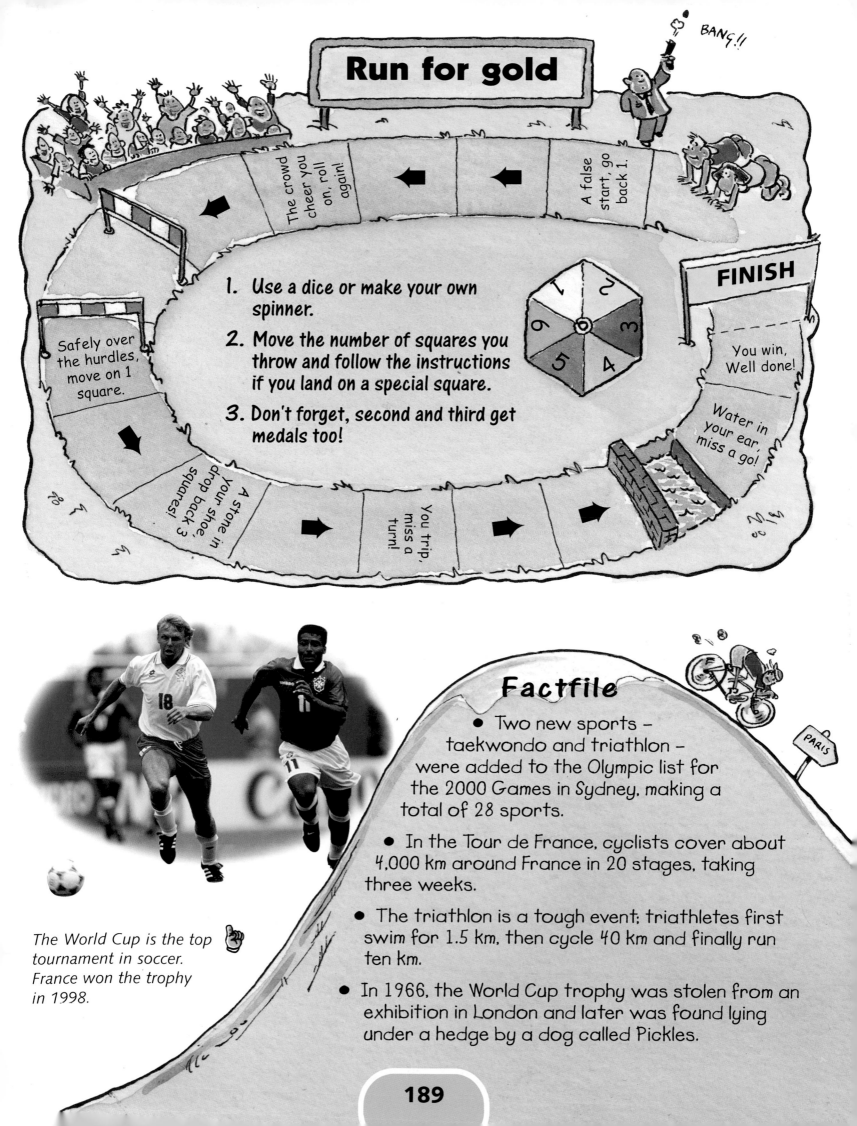

Run for gold

BANG!!

The crowd cheer you on, roll again!

A false start, go back 1.

FINISH

You win, Well done!

1. Use a dice or make your own spinner.

2. Move the number of squares you throw and follow the instructions if you land on a special square.

3. Don't forget, second and third get medals too!

Safely over the hurdles, move on 1 square.

Water in your ear, miss a go!

A stone in your shoe in drop back 3 squares!

You trip, miss a turn!

The World Cup is the top tournament in soccer. France won the trophy in 1998.

Factfile

• Two new sports – taekwondo and triathlon – were added to the Olympic list for the 2000 Games in Sydney, making a total of 28 sports.

• In the Tour de France, cyclists cover about 4,000 km around France in 20 stages, taking three weeks.

• The triathlon is a tough event; triathletes first swim for 1.5 km, then cycle 40 km and finally run ten km.

• In 1966, the World Cup trophy was stolen from an exhibition in London and later was found lying under a hedge by a dog called Pickles.

PARIS

Index